AF305273

Nejat Satı

Nejat Satı

Color as Psychological Balance

edited by Necmi Sönmez

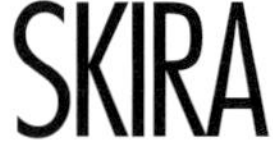
SKIRA

Cover
Wound / Nefs series
2022
Acrylic and heavy gel on canvas
60 × 100 cm
(detail)

Design
Anna Cattaneo

Editorial Coordination
Eva Vanzella

Copy Editor
Carlotta Santuccio

Layout
Beba Pineschi

Translations
Müge Atala
Ayşe Draz

Photo Credits
Nazlı Erdemirel
Ramazan Tunç

First published in Italy in 2022 by
Skira editore S.p.A.
Palazzo Casati Stampa
via Torino 61
20123 Milano
Italy
www.skira.net

Printed and bound in Italy. First edition

ISBN: 978-88-572-4592-8

Distributed in USA, Canada, Central
& South America by ARTBOOK | D.A.P.
75 Broad Street, Suite 630, New York,
NY 10004, USA.
Distributed elsewhere in the world by
Thames and Hudson Ltd., 181A High Holborn,
London WC1V 7QX, United Kingdom.

Contents

The Memory of Colors and the Body in Nejat Satı's Paintings

Necmi Sönmez

"I've waited so long I don't even have a minute now." This sentence frequently repeated by Nejat Satı (fig. 1) during our project meetings with him whose small atelier I frequently visited in Büyük Kardıçalı Han as I was preparing the Port İzmir Triennial in 2009, for some reason, stuck in my mind. As far as I could see, he was the most experimental, most elusive and unpredictable representative of his generation. While closely observing his works, I struggled to understand Nejat's impatience as he undertook unexpected experiments by taking the color element as his point of departure in his painting, sculpture, and three-dimensional works. Our first collaboration with Nejat, who realized dynamizing actions with his artist friends and worked non-stop in this city where life and art flow harmoniously, was in 2010. It didn't take me long to realize that there were differences between Nejat whom I witnessed how meticulously, carefully, and even worshipfully pit his shoulder to the wheel while working on *Aden Municipality Park and Garden Work. We Apologize for the Inconvenience Caused to Our People. Aden Municipality* (*Aden Belediyesi Park ve Bahçe Çalışması. Halkımıza verdiğimiz rahatsızlıktan dolayı özür dileriz. Aden Belediyesi*) (fig. 2) and the artist of his

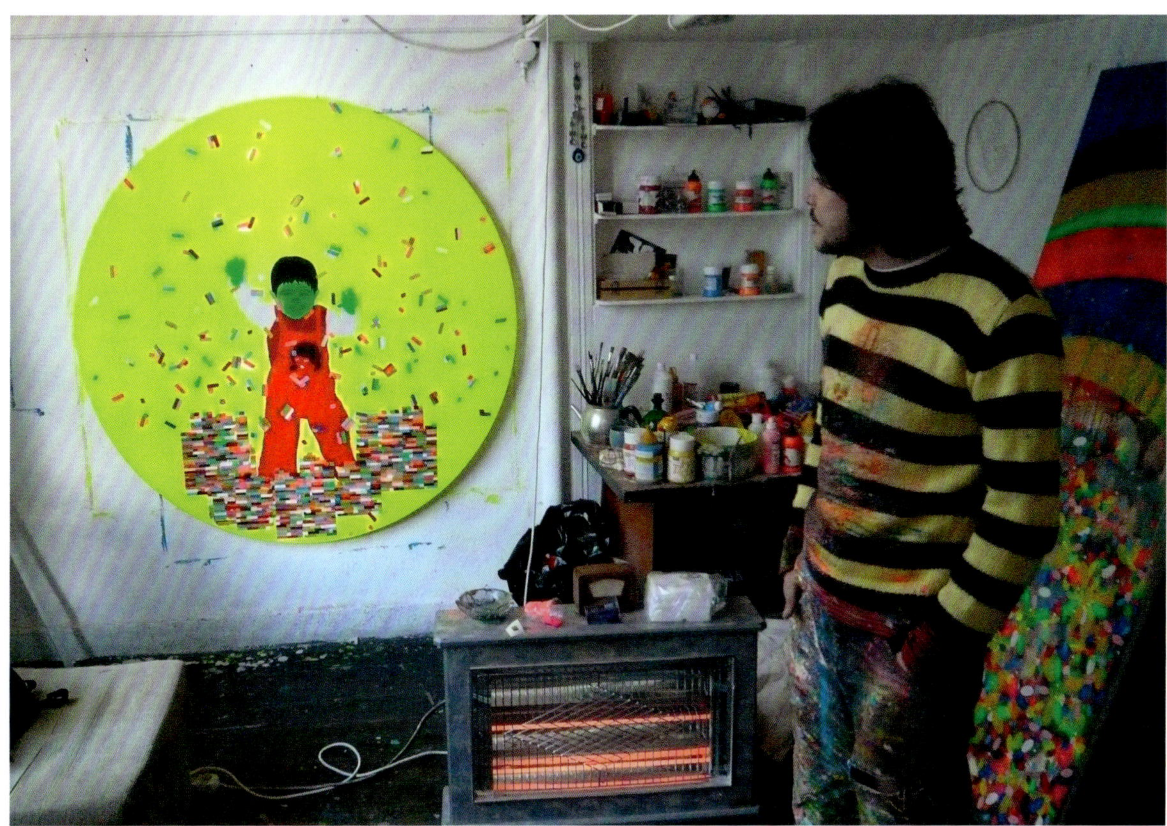

1. Nejat Satı, Büyük Kardıçalı Han atelier, İzmir, 2009
Photo: Necmi Sönmez

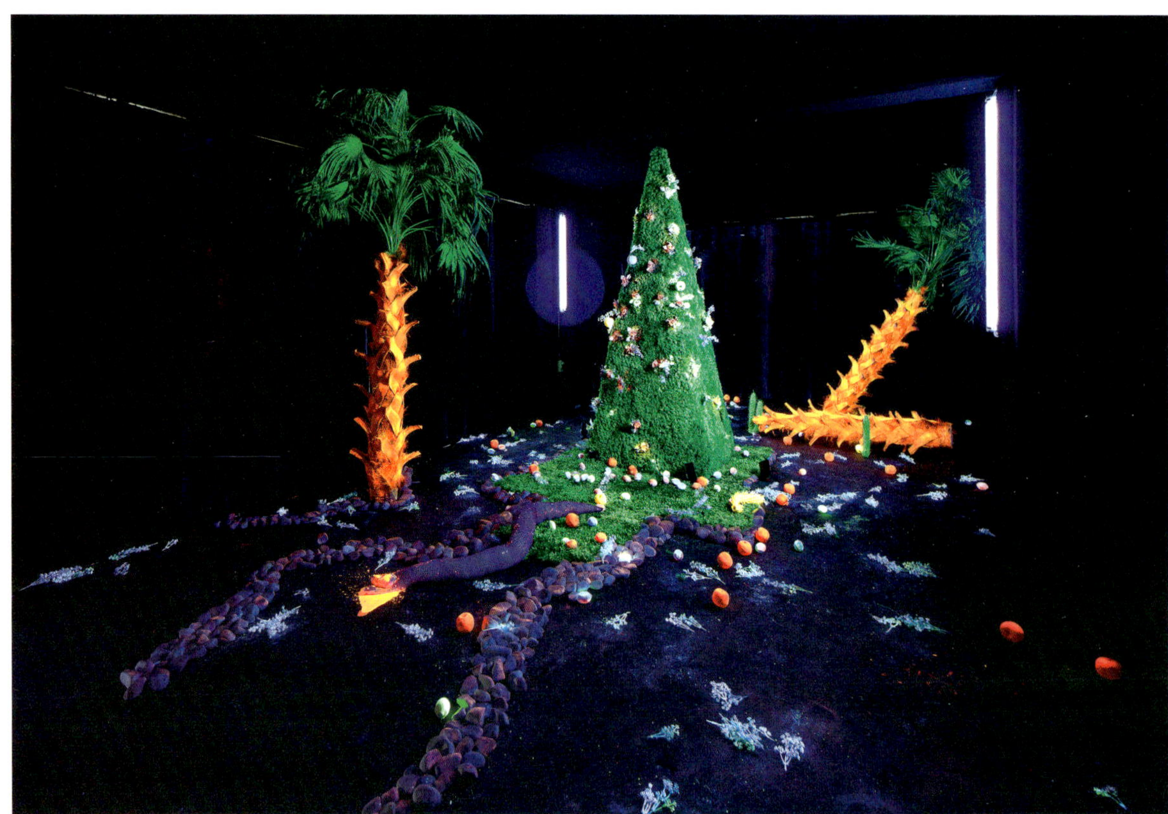

radiant, eye-catching paintings where all sorts of colors flash and sparkle. Focusing on colors that made their difference felt at first sight, Nejat had by then started to develop his own signature at a very early age by concentrating on forms resembling different pills and medicine capsules. There was a huge difference between the artist of these canvases, which radiated joy, happiness, and delight, and Nejat, whom I was just getting to know. Although the fact that he came from a family of pharmacists would suffice to explain the origins of forms in his glittering universe such as pills, capsules, and suppositories, I sensed from our conversations over time that there were different realities behind Nejat's work, but I could not bring myself to ask him about it. Because we didn't really know each other.

In addition to the annual group exhibitions, we developed two different site-specific projects with Nejat, who came to Istanbul from İzmir to participate in the workshop program at ArtCenter/Istanbul in 2010.[1] The first of these was *Chopin Nocturne Op. 9 No. 2* (fig. 3) for the Borusan Music Library, which was active at the time, and the other was a site-specific work for the *Elgiz 10* exhibition in 2011, on the wall where Fahrelnissa Zeid's paintings were exhibited (fig. 4). I was able to witness the psychological universe behind the vibrant color combinations of Nejat's paintings, during these projects seeking different forms of expression other than canvas painting.

Although the identity that colors—which express the joy of living—assume in Nejat's works is closely related to the Simultanism,[2] Monochrome,[3] and Colorfield-Painting[4] movements appearing in different periods of modern and contemporary art, it also deviates from them, being shaped by the psychological perception of the audience and taking on different identities at different times. This particular quality is characterized by a melancholic aspect that I discussed in detail in an article I wrote in 2010.[5] Since then, Nejat has developed a visual expression based on abstract elements in five different series that have often developed and intertwined with each other with clear beginnings yet uncertain endings. Before looking into these series more closely, however, I would like to discuss three significant works that I think contain extremely important clues as to what the "psychological aspects of colors" are or might be that play a key role in Nejat's art. I am referring to *The Girl Who Spills Her Antidepressants on the Floor While Eating Her Hot Dog at the Hairdresser* (*Kuaförde Sosislisini Yerken Antidepresanlarını Yere Döken Kız*, 2008) (fig. 5), *The Boy Knocking Over Legos* (*Legoları Yıkan Çoçuk*, 2009), and *Self-Portrait: Child on a Donkey* (*Otoportre: Eşek Üzerindeki Çoçuk*, 2010) (fig. 6). Both abstract and figurative elements stand out in these early period paintings, yet, upon careful observation, their compositional arrangement reveals uncertainties, uncanny, and even repulsive elements that seem strange to the viewer and only emerge after looking at them for a while. For example, the viewer is unable to see that the girl eating the hot dog and the boy who knocks down his Legos are both representations of the artist trying to overcome the depression of puberty. It would not be far-fetched to describe them as the artist's struggle between existence and extinction, the crises he experienced while creating his unique painting language. These three paintings summarize the troubled relationships that a young artist, having opened his first solo exhibition in 2009 (*Well done* [*Aferin*], Apartment Project, Istanbul), has established with himself, his family, the environment he grew up in, the friends he socialized with, and with the professional art world he finally stepped into, as he was tearing his pictorial cocoon and weaving it over and over again.

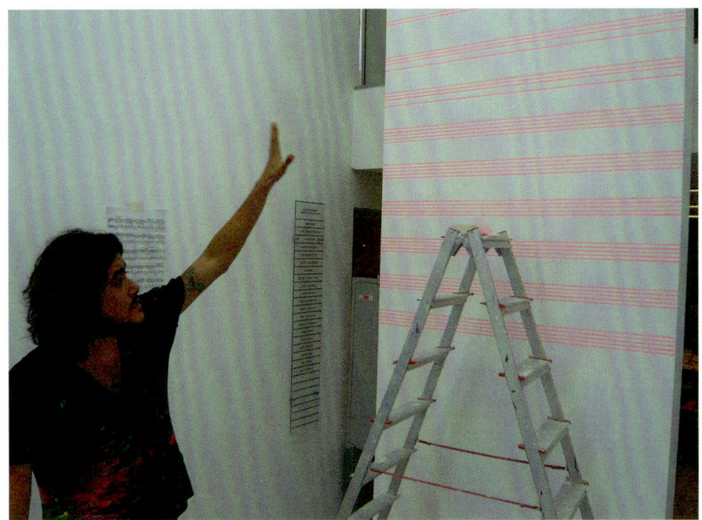

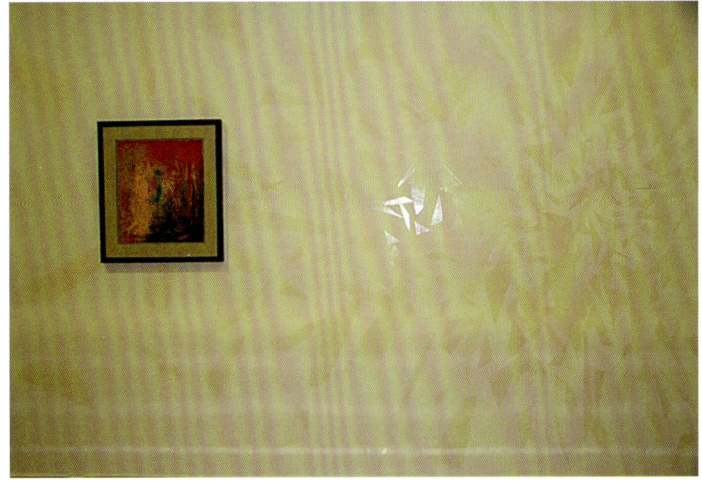

3. Nejat Satı with *Chopin Nocturne Op. 9 No. 2*, Borusan Music Library, 2010
Photo: Necmi Sönmez

4. Site-specific wall installation with a work by Fahrelnissa Zeid, Elgiz Museum, 2011
Photo: Necmi Sönmez

Artists walk in all sorts of paths. Sometimes they take repeated steps in the same rhythm. Sometimes they compare with others. Nejat wanders through the memories of his childhood toy he always kept by, the sheets he slept on (fig. 7), the streets he played in, the school gardens he attended, the wooden school desks in which he sat bored witless (fig. 8), the lights in the sky, the scents swirling around ripe figs, in short, through the traces that seem to be part of a large encrypted script of early youth spent in the Aegean. Even the daily conversations of family members, who are pharmacists and doctors, are full of keywords that can solve the miraculous language of drugs. Nejat senses the grammar of this miracle already when he was a child through colors to which he attributes different meanings. Red stands for healing, green scares, yellow stuns. However, Nejat's childlike intuitions refuse to take a concrete form when he decides to become an artist in his youth and to be the key to fully decipher the code called "healing." Because, like disease, healing is also shaped by human desires and thoughts. In such moments of intensification, colors have energies that they spread around and psychological intuitions. They maintain their existence in flows that are sensed and felt, but not seen.

The eye sees colors but does not comprehend at once. Because the emotional intensity of the eye cannot reach the speed of the brain in understanding. In those moments, the qualities of colors re-moving psychological barriers and being remolded with emotions such as happiness, sadness, pain, are filled with the truth of being human. As the symphony of the universe this the subject of the "eye of the heart," not of the "eye that sees." Nejat is an artist whose series of paintings are constructed on the psychological adjustments of color and who goes after moments that can be sensed by those who look with enthusiasm and faith. A psychological framework shaped by the imaginary intersections of emotion and perception has preserved its existence in his series first shaped in Urla, İzmir, and later in Istanbul, Düsseldorf, and Bozburun.

The common feature of these series, which I will soon discuss in more detail, is that the energies formed by the color combinations are composed of rotating, moving masses. As these masses are separated from all appearances of nature and transformed into abstract forms of existence, they bear witness to the struggle that Nejat has embarked upon over the last ten years. So, let us now witness how they have evolved nonlinearly, going further and further into eluding crystalline, vegetal forms. Although they have different names, with the concept-meaning coherence they have established, these series provide detailed information about the pictorial themes that Nejat has focused on since he was a student, as well as the psychological aspects of the colors he developed with his unique techniques. Speaking of which, it must be emphasized that the colors Nejat creates by mixing different materials with the meticulousness of an alchemist are not bought in shops selling art supplies, but are colors that the artist produces by experimenting, mixing, and examining their reactions over a long period of time. These colors, which with their phosphoric properties appear differently in daylight, under electric light or in complete darkness, take on different characters in Nejat's series.

Organic Abstract, 2008

What is a painting? This question, which has been attempted to be answered time and again in the light of developments in the art world since the 1980s, is closely related to how colors are applied on the canvas. Indeed, this subject, which has been on the art world's agenda since the beginning of the nineteenth century, is today closely related to how canvas painting develops

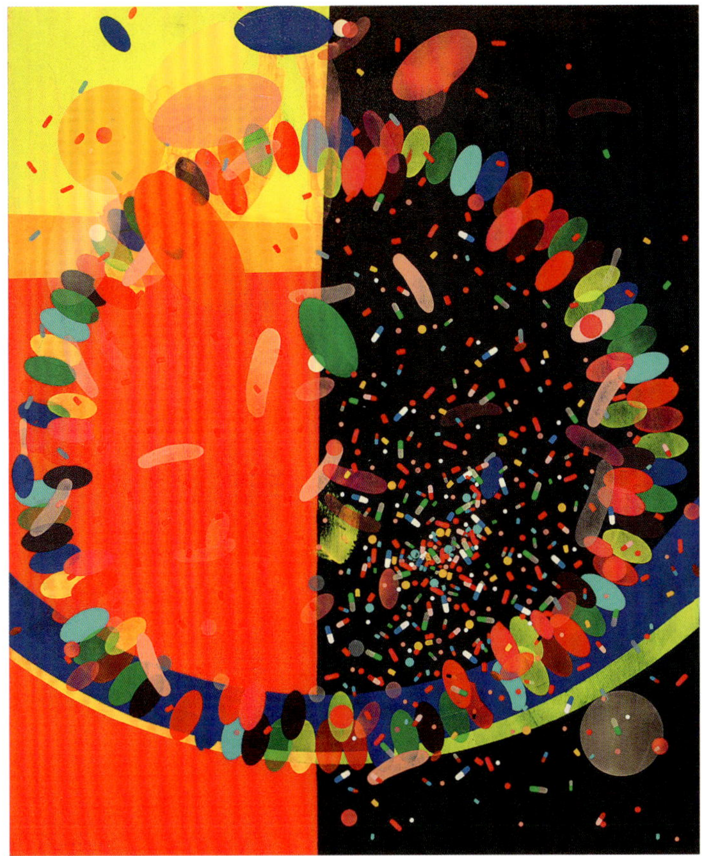

an attitude towards digital perception. In his paintings created since 2009, Nejat has insisted on advancing along the lines of canvas painting since he, before anything else as a representative of the generation in which digital experiences were shaped, sought to answer the question of what painting is with the benefits of different screen experiences (computer, iPad, mobile phone, etc.). Having long researched how the canvas responds to digital observations, Nejat has found his own way with his instincts since the time in 2008 when he started experimenting with different materials with phosphoric effects. What interests him is closely related to the question of how his paintings will open the door to an ongoing visual experience. Because Nejat decides the fate of his canvases with his own hands, without the help of an assistant. It is obvious that his compositions are shaped by the decisions made when the paint is transferred and applied to the canvas surface. Although the *Organic Abstract* series originates in 2008 from the pill-shaped "small circles," it would not be wrong to argue that this series derives from pixels. Forms observed in the works from this series at the end evolve into pixels, which are the smallest homogeneous units in colors that make up the digital image. Nejat turns these forms, and the color textures he creates with his unique material mixtures as he changes both the dimensions of the pixels and the shapes of the canvases, into his visual signature.

They have a "bodily" character which refers to the rounded human body forms in the *Organic Abstract* series. The inter-relationship of the circles, spread on the canvas surface with the help of a special knife, is shaped by "color experiences." The monochrome tones in these circles, even though they suggest "optical events,"[6] as they vibrate when they get close to one another, can perhaps be considered in a musical context. Innovations might be seen in the forms that Nejat revisits with his impressive color combinations, but there are no repetitions. Because the circles that characterize this series, whether in large or very small forms, have a calmness that gives the painting integrity.

Melancholia, 2012

The integrity of the composition is one of the basic phenomena that we encounter in the works Nejat has produced since his student years. In his works from the *Melancholia* series, which Nejat has developed since 2012, this holistic expression transforms the painting surface into areas that are sometimes permeable-opaque, sometimes broken, fragmented and transparentized in various colors. This allows Nejat to evoke the human body without giving up on abstract expression. It is no coincidence that this series, which he first developed using acrylic paint and then the transparent gel material he produced with his own unique mixtures, metaphorically evokes bodies that have received a blow and have undergone surgery. The construction of surfaces that can be defined as "under the skin" or "above the skin," as the references present in the *Organic Abstract* series to red blood cells in the blood now refer to the human body in this series, is an important victory for Nejat in his relentless war with color. Because the artist, while using the limited possibilities of abstract expression, creates a sea of perception by engaging in such strange experiments on the painting surface created by putting or, bluntly said, by piling one thing on top of another so that it is not immediately clear which color is in the foreground and which in the background. Nejat succeeds in transforming the painting surface he creates with a significant struggle into a sensitive and subtle space, and shapes it with "all-over"[7] and camouflage techniques, as if weaving a carpet, paying attention to its every centimeter. This richness of expression is also diversified by the pigments circulating in the gel material, and opaque surfaces evoke metaphors such as sickness and fragility.

It is a must to talk about the dramaturgy of colors in the paintings of this series, which reveal the importance of the painting surface in Nejat's artistic adventure. The densities observed sometimes in the center, sometimes at the edges of the composition, as well as the opaque areas representing an optical fragmentation and rupture, are closely related to the psychological effects that colors arouse in the audience.

Structure, 2012

The "expression" that is constructed with color blocks which come on top and under one another without any brush trace is striking in the *Structure* series, emphasizing the importance of the edges of the composition as well as the surface of the painting.

The "transparency," which sometimes comes to the fore and sometimes stays in the background of the color blocks shaped by the rapid movements of Nejat on the canvas without relying on a certain sketch or pre-study, not only creates spatial distances from the painting surface, but also draws the viewer's attention deeper, giving the works in this series a privileged character.

The "sense of depth" achieved without creating any illusion of perspective on the painting surface, has, at first glance, a reverse relationship with the color blocks and particles that overflow these compositions. So, as the viewer gets closer to the work, the sense of depth s/he perceives increases and s/he begins to see the bumpy perimeters of gel particles spilling out of the composition. It is as if Nejat left these pieces overflowing from the canvas for the watchful eyes to notice the paths they

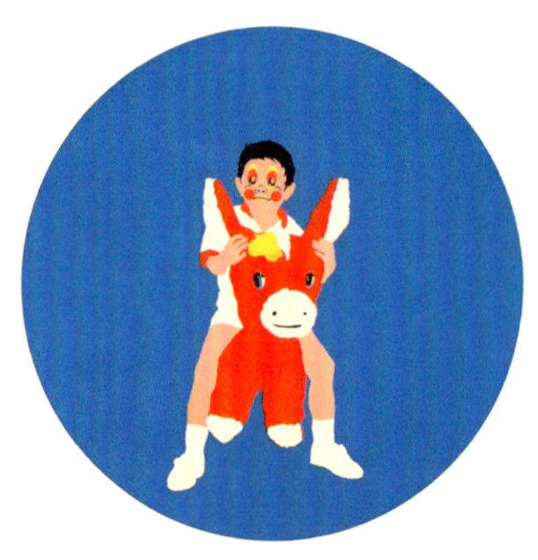

6. *Self-Portrait: Child on a Donkey*, 2010, private collection
Photo: Nejat Satı Studio, Istanbul

7. *Artist's Childhood Bed Linen*, 1985

8. *Painted School Desk*, 2010–12,
acrylic on wood, 50 × 40 cm,
private collection

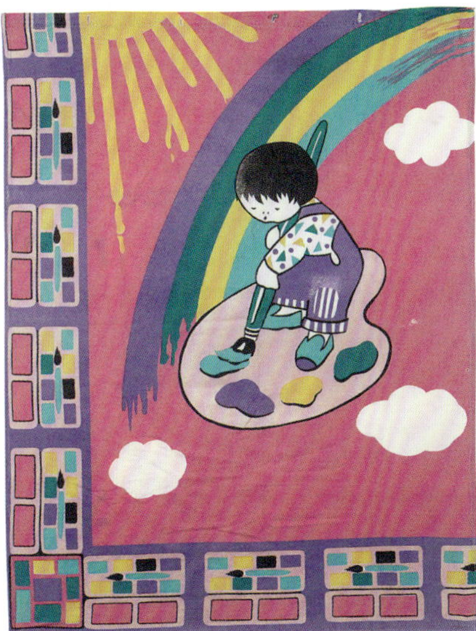 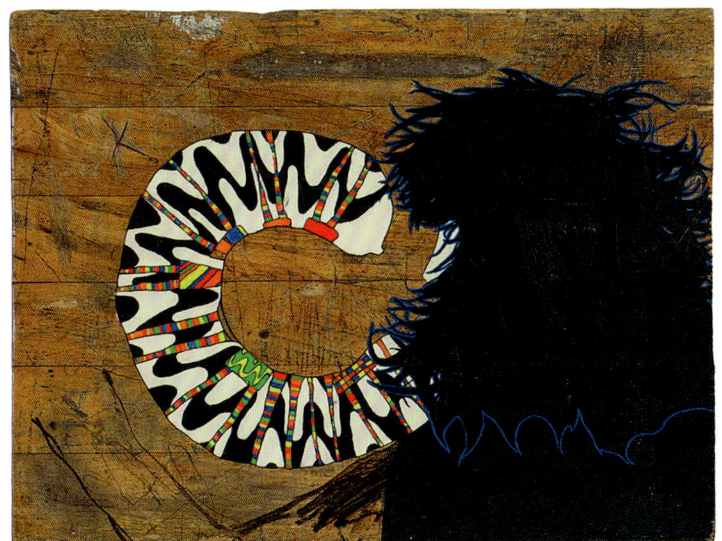

pass. While in the previous series the way in which the movement of the canvas surface is created remains somewhat sealed,[8] the particles overflowing from the edges in *Structure* are full of details that reveal which colors the artist uses to create the color blocks and how he progresses one by one. These particles which, upon first glance, may raise the question of why the artist has not cleaned them, reveal both how the color is applied to the canvas and the "spatial relation" dialog formed by each color block with the previous one.

Since the "spatial relations" are often triggered by monochromatic or limited use of color in this series, the paintings open the doors for the audience to different feelings of depth-lightness, even flying and ascension. Nejat himself tends to break the spell of the painting in this series where he highlights the relationship between the composition itself and the parts that overflow the frame, without belittling the experiences of those who followed the same path before him. He does not believe in the difference of the artist, in the fairy tale that s/he will work wonders when s/he takes the brush in her/his hand. He makes the viewer look at the painting with bated breath as he displays how the layers of color overlap, with an open-heartedness revealing how he works in this series.

In this way the viewer, while witnessing how the depths of color, the inner movement, and the dynamism in the mid-tones are formed, shares a common fate with the act of painting (Akt des Malens). The gel and pigment residues overflowing from the peripheries of the painting become landmarks of different points of view for both the artist and the viewer.

Nefs (*Nafs*), 2013

Nafs, a word of Arabic origin, is a concept that has twenty different worldly and religious meanings including primarily psyche, ego, soul, self, mind, body, corpse, blood, grandeur, bad wishes.[9] Nejat had started this series during the Gezi Protests which took place between May 28 and August 30, 2013, after seeing photos of participants' and supporters' bodies that had taken a blow published via social media channels, in the wake of the issue surrounding police brutality.[10] During this period, Nejat had come to a new crossroads, on the one hand, going back and forth between two cities due to his preparations to return from Istanbul to İzmir, and, on the other hand, trying to give a different direction to the experiences he gained from all his previous series. In his paintings of the *Nafs* series, which coincides with a kind of purification process in his artistic journey, the colors that are predominantly purple or close to purple have different meanings and aspects. The first of these is undoubtedly the "body."

For Nejat, who in his early works interpreted the human figure with references from his own biography to his childhood and adolescence, the body did not have a schematic, representational feature. In the *Nafs* series, he has considered the body as a concept to be discovered based on the details, not on the visible, since he grasped figure in the line consisting of all experiences, and he shaped this series with a kind of internal reckoning.

The bruises that form on the bodies that have taken a blow, and which maintain their impact for a long time, form the memory of the individual who has been exposed to violence as traces of "experienced pain." Nejat is in pursuit of contrasts as never before in this series, which he focused on particularly between 2013 and 2016 when he returned from Istanbul to İzmir seeking new directions for himself. The "dramaturgy of pain," which he tries to reflect without using sixth elements, finds its most impressive expression with the juxtaposition of warm and cold color tones without the need for intermediate zones. Indeed, the contrasts formed by the combination of red and blue, yellow and green can be compared to "silent screams." It is not a coincidence that the tableaux surface is rough in the paintings within this series, which Nejat developed based on a social revolt and worked on repeatedly over the years. The textures, that attentive eyes would discover in a short while and which evoke Istanbul's bumpy streets that cannot be leveled despite being asphalted many times, add an impressive dynamism to all these works.

Catharsis, 2020

Nejat, who does not progress on a temporal and spatial plane in either his personal life or his series, followed a stream of life that went the opposite direction from what was expected, as he moved his workshop in Urla to Istanbul at a time when the onset of the Covid-19 pandemic turned life upside down and people living in the metropolises were migrating to villages and towns. It is not yet clear how the *Catharsis* series, which he shaped upon his return to the metropolis, will develop, since he began it in 2020 but continues to work on it into 2022. But the six years Nejat spent between 2014 and 2020, most of the time in rural solitude, on the shores of the sea which he loved since childhood, in the artichoke and lotus gardens, can be considered as a kind of rejuvenation process. Although he has developed exhibitions quite effectively both in Turkey and abroad during this time, it is obvious that his retreat has created a certain accumulation for what he wants to do in the future. The *Catharsis* series, which is the expression of this accumulation, consists of touching compositions that Nejat constructs by entering an inner purification process in his own world of form and color.

It is not by accident that in the works from this series certain points of focus are created by dividing the canvas surface into horizontal sections. Nejat has succeeded in creating light sensitive areas on the canvas surface by forcing his visual experiences, which he gathered from his previous series, into new associations, in these compositions resembling the pictograms on the Babylonian, Assyrian horizontal seals. In the *Catharsis* series, the light should be handled in a different way, as it comes out of the colors used by the artist, not from a certain corner in the classical sense.

The "fields/islands of light" appearing, just as in the early works of the *Organic Abstract* series, in forms reminiscent of drug capsules among the impressive color blocks in the paintings of this series, do not only indicate "emotional purification" as the name of the series suggests. In the works from this series, the phenomenon of light refers to hope, which is the expression of the "inner voice" that defends the correctness of their beliefs under all circumstances. Impressive "clusters of light," whose origins and how they fell on the canvas are unclear, are the last and perhaps one of the most uncertain landmarks in Nejat's artistic process.

One of the reasons why I care about Nejat's fast-paced series that he developed over a period of nearly fifteen years, often without looking back, is that these works have the potential to wipe out many misunderstandings in our art history with a boring past repeating only a few graphic skills for a lifetime. I think that they descended to earth from another world since I know their smells and textures, having seen them many times, both in the Büyük Kardıçalı Inn and the workshop in Altunizade, during daytime, in the electric light, in daylight, and in the dark. These series, which will be enjoyed by eyes that see under all circumstances, have a magic that goes beyond the visible with their physical and psychological aspects. More importantly, they develop their own reality by resisting the flow and standstill of time.

1 ArtCenter/Istanbul was the first support program in Turkey, established in 2009–13 with the idea and support of Ahmet Kocabıyık, to provide ateliers to young people with an art education after their graduation. As the curator, I was preparing an exhibition of current productions every year within the framework of this project.

2 The concept of "Simultaneous," developed in 1913 by Blaise Cendrars (1887–1961) and Sonia Delaunay-Terk (1885–1978), played an important role in the development process of modern art.

3 When I say Monochrome, I refer to the color-oriented creative processes that started with Kazimir Malevich, and after being crowned by Yves Klein developed with Robert Ryman, Robert Mangold, David Novros, Gerhard Richter, Ulrich Erben, and Marcia Light, continuing their influence into today.

4 In the concept of "Colorfield Painting" developed by Clement Greenberg (1909–1994), the phenomenon of pure color appears as a result of an abstraction that avoids all references.

5 Necmi Sönmez, "Melancholy in the Triangle of Color Form Dream: On Nejat Satı's Works," in *Nejat Satı: Hâlet-i Ruhiye, Dilaltı / State of Mind* (Istanbul: Pi Artworks, 2012). Exhibition catalog.

6 When the Istanbulite painter Albert Bitran (1929–2018) went to Paris in 1948, he participated in group exhibitions with representatives of the movement, which would later be named Op-Art, such as Victor Vasarely and Rafael Jesus Soto. When talking about his paintings in this style, which he later abandoned, Albert preferred the term "optical event."

7 The "all-over" technique is closely related to evoking in the viewer a sense of continuity that can be repeated indefinitely on a two-dimensional plane of the painting surface without making reference to a certain motif. It refers to many of Cy Twombly's paintings as well as being closely related to Jackson Pollack's *Drip-Paintings* and Mark Tobey's *Abstract Calligraphy* series.

8 From a private conversation with the artist, January 4, 2020.

9 https://en.wikipedia.org/wiki/Nafs (accessed January 26, 2022).

10 From a private conversation with the artist, January 17, 2020.

Nejat Satı: Painting as a Self-Talk with the Other

Sabine Maria Schmidt

It is difficult to become an abstract image. In everything we recognize things and phenomena that seem familiar, we see traces and experiences of sounds, spaces, colors, and light in images. A great deal of discipline is therefore required.

In concrete art or radical abstract painting, its producers voluntarily enter a relatively narrow space of investigation. Their field of work is precisely defined. The artists subject themselves to rigid restrictions that actually seem to contradict the freedom of means that painting offers in principle. This is especially true for monochrome painting, which usually focuses on the effect of color as material (with specific properties). Thus, abstract painting is usually somehow more modest than figurative painting. "One consequence of such conceptual radicality is that concrete or monochrome painting can legitimize itself through nothing but itself: where the painting neither appears as an image of something nor stands for something else, in an abstract or symbolic sense, than what it is concretely, only its being-so-made and its effect remain the criteria for its meaning," art historian Michael Fehr once wrote. Therefore, abstract painting is usually somehow more autistic than figurative painting.

First of all, Nejat Satı's painting is never "concrete"—if we stand by the definition of Concrete Art introduced by Theo van Doesburg, which is based on constructivist principles and mostly basic geometric forms. It is not fully designed or shaped.

Nonetheless, Nejat Satı's painting, too, stands for itself. It is both a means and a subject. Above all, it is not much: perhaps expressive or virtuosic, fast or slow, romantic or rational. Such dialectical opposites are even noticeably renounced. Yet his painting—like all painting—is also a medium of communication. Each layer of paint is superimposed on top of another and thus reacts to the previous one. In this sense, Satı's painting is a self-talk with itself but also with the other.

Still, one can find in the art of Nejat Satı various approaches and echoes of abstract image strategies. Satı titled a 2009 painting *Bacterium*, which shows a proliferating multiplication of vividly swarming colored bodies. In the context of his works, it is a striking image, since it also explicitly inquires about the independence of painting, negating representation in the transition from the figurative to the abstract. And it is a small farewell to an essential component of artistic compositions, the line that Satı seems to renounce in his radical abstraction and later series of works.

A first draft, a small sketch, a noted thought usually begins with a line. This simple, one-dimensional graphic element opens up a multifaceted panorama of aesthetic forms. "A line is a dot that went for a walk," said Paul Klee, who precisely examined the essence of the line as an independent means on the path to abstraction. He compares the genesis of a drawing with a walk through free nature. The line was also a central design element for representatives of the constructivist avant-garde, with which forms and geometries could be utilized for pictorial compositions according to mathematical laws.

Last but not least, three-dimensional object constructions were also formed. The subjective expression of an artist's handwriting that manifested in the line was replaced by circles and mechanical drawing devices.

In contrast to pure surfaces and color compositions, the confrontation of lines and contours in painting is a classic introduction to its craftsmanship. A line fulfills a multitude of functions: it sets boundaries, defines forms, draws on or after, creates a temporality and structure (as in the watercolors of Paul Klee), and allows space-dynamic effects to be produced. Satı also creates spatial dynamics in his painting *Bacterium*, where he lets the rod-like lineatures become greater from layer to layer, thus allowing them to "grow." There are virtually no painted lines themselves, however.

The view of the image has become a kind of view through a microscope in his works since 2012. Satı dips the color pigments in a specific gel-like solution and allows the color material to expand itself. *Hemoglobin* (2012) is one of the first works in the new series *Organic*, which can be read in a way as painting research. This work creates monochrome pictorial spatialities in which liquid drop shapes appear to solidify into round circles. Some image compositions are somewhat reminiscent of school experiments in which agar, bacteria, and yeasts would grow in Petri dishes based on the jelly-like substance.

In addition to monochrome paintings, there are also several multicolored works in which color theory and color teaching are incorporated. In these chromatic constellations, light manifests itself through subtle color sounds that set the image surface in vibration. One can compare this approach of Nejat Satı with that of German artist Peter Zimmermann. In his work, Zimmermann initially dealt in particular with the question of originals and copies and the subject of reproduction. This theme can also be found in his pop-like "candy painting," which was developed to perfection, as I would like to call the epoxy resin works, which sometimes remind of children's lollipops. Over the years, Zimmermann has repeatedly developed new series of works while also remaining faithful to his subject of reproduction. In a large-format work entitled *Liquid*, for example, photographs and film stills are digitally enlarged and edited so that the original figure is hardly recognizable. The resulting motif structures are applied to the canvas in several layers with epoxy resin and transformed into an enormously color-intensive image body. Zimmermann's high-gloss paintings are abstract images that also deal with image-making in the age of digital reproducibility. At times they are based on the ubiquitously seductive presence of high-resolution plasma screens.

Nejat Satı also formally conserves picturesque phenomena in his gel-like color materiality. Crystalline structures are formed in a series he names *Catharsis*. As if the fragmented, the destroyed, or the alien in these fascinating picturesque kaleidoscopes wanted to embrace themselves and free themselves from destructive conflicts. Due to the depths and layers, it is not easy to optically reconstruct how the works are formed. In all of the paintings, however, something seems to be captured and finally banned in its destructive effectiveness. The squeegee and scraping marks, which the artist uses here instead of a classic brush, develop a life of their own. Or is it the scraped-in spiritual life of the artist that is frozen here? One would almost be tempted to read the entire series of *Melancholia* paintings as brittle glass windows. Some appear to be highly fragile and focus in perspective on a predetermined breaking point. Others, especially the red ones, seem to be splintered, but at the same time

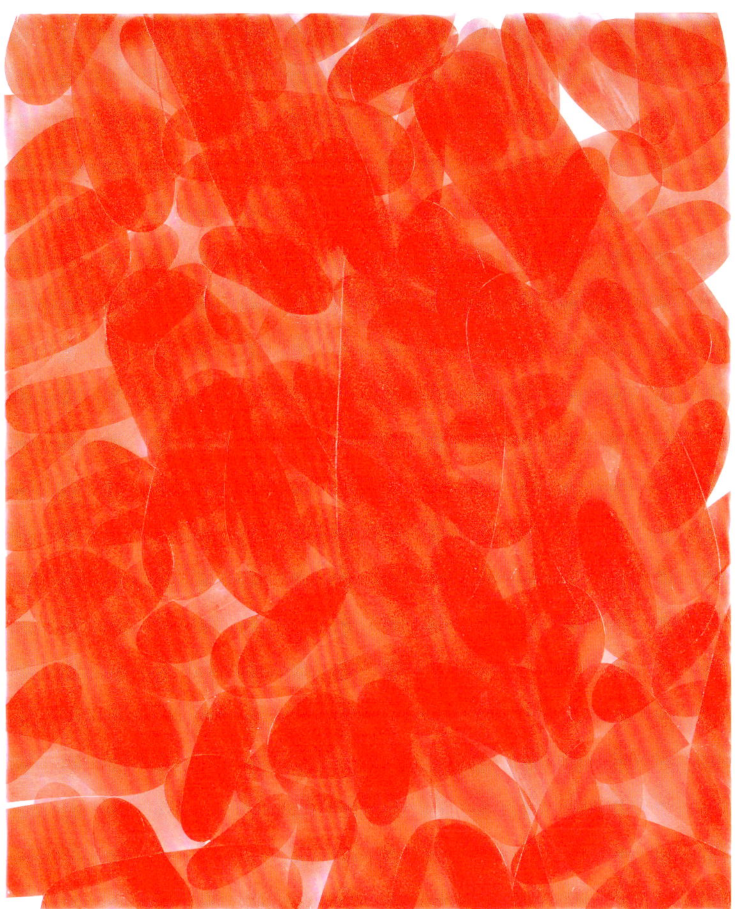

1. *Hemoglobin / Organic* series, 2012,
acrylic and heavy gel on canvas,
160 × 150 cm

they grow together again to form beautiful ornaments. Oblivious ornamental forms and color gradients appearing vegetatively are lost in the pictorial space. They are images that turn to their own interior, which can even lead into a deep black hole (as in *Beyaz Boşluk*, 2016). Or they transform themselves into an exploding, fantastically colored firebird (*Catharsis* series, 2020–21). But enough now, the figurative has nothing to do here.

It cannot be excluded that Nejat Satı is also inspired for his different groups of works by other artists and motifs of different origins, but he always seems to follow the opposite path. First he creates an effect and then he looks. In his more extensive series of *Structures*, Satı literally works against the decorative favor that arises too quickly in his organic color circle images. Only indistinctly can structures be recognized among the increasingly dense layers of color, which resemble rather blurred, dreamlike images of memory. Nothing is as obvious in painting as painting one layer on top of another, superimposing one image over another. And yet this method offers fascinating facets and possibilities for differentiating between painting and colored bodies.

Above all, the series of *Structures* contains many self-talks with the other. Even abstract or strongly abstracted images themselves are characterized by numerous recognition effects. It does not always have to be Mark Rothko who serves as a term of comparison. Some pictorial bodies are reminiscent of the works of German painter Rupprecht Geiger, others of the wax layers of Polke or Sybille Pattscheck. Here, something seems to have emerged that was previously hidden. Light penetrates from the inside out. In other images, as in palimpsests, layers seem to be painted over one another, as if something had to be concealed. Painting remains a constant process of trying to negotiate and balance. Is an image as it should be? Did the painter finish the work as he intended to paint it? Is there such a controlled process at all? This is difficult for the observer to recapitulate. Some paintings like *Isimsiz* end up like a "stream of consciousness."

While in some paintings Satı leaves the interaction between color material and image carrier to chance and merely controls the relationship between the gelatinous mass and color, in others he seems to rework the structures in a more controlled manner. In the *Structure* series, many paintings stand out in which the color surface, like ceramic glaze, seem to merge with the image carrier and content. Especially in *Nefs*, the image surfaces condense into opaque glazes. The joy of playing with color light and reflections is obvious. Bringing light sources into these textures, even burning them in and making them shine from the inside, is an effect that can also be read out again for us viewers. As with glazes, Nejat Satı tests chromatic constellations. Light manifests itself through subtle color sounds. Among others, the word *Nefs* can be translated as "spirit" and "self." Some of the particularly beautiful and colored pieces are reminiscent of chromatic thermal images and also allude to spiritual emotions or psychological effects of color. Here one can find all the bright colors such as blue, yellow, red, and green.

Normally, art history is imagined as a linear consequence of artistic achievements that build on each other. At the top stands always the very latest (the avant-garde), from where one can see everything one has seen in the rear-view mirror. This perspective has become routine, it is believed that one already knows the individual stations by heart. Only in recent years has there been a departure from such a linear view, which is based on a determinant idea of progress. The world has become increasingly rhizomatic.

No classical work development can be reconstructed in the work of Nejat Satı either. There are numerous parallel approaches, which are repeatedly questioned and continued by Satı. Thus, there is always something anachronistic attached to his works, since a wide variety of painting research and

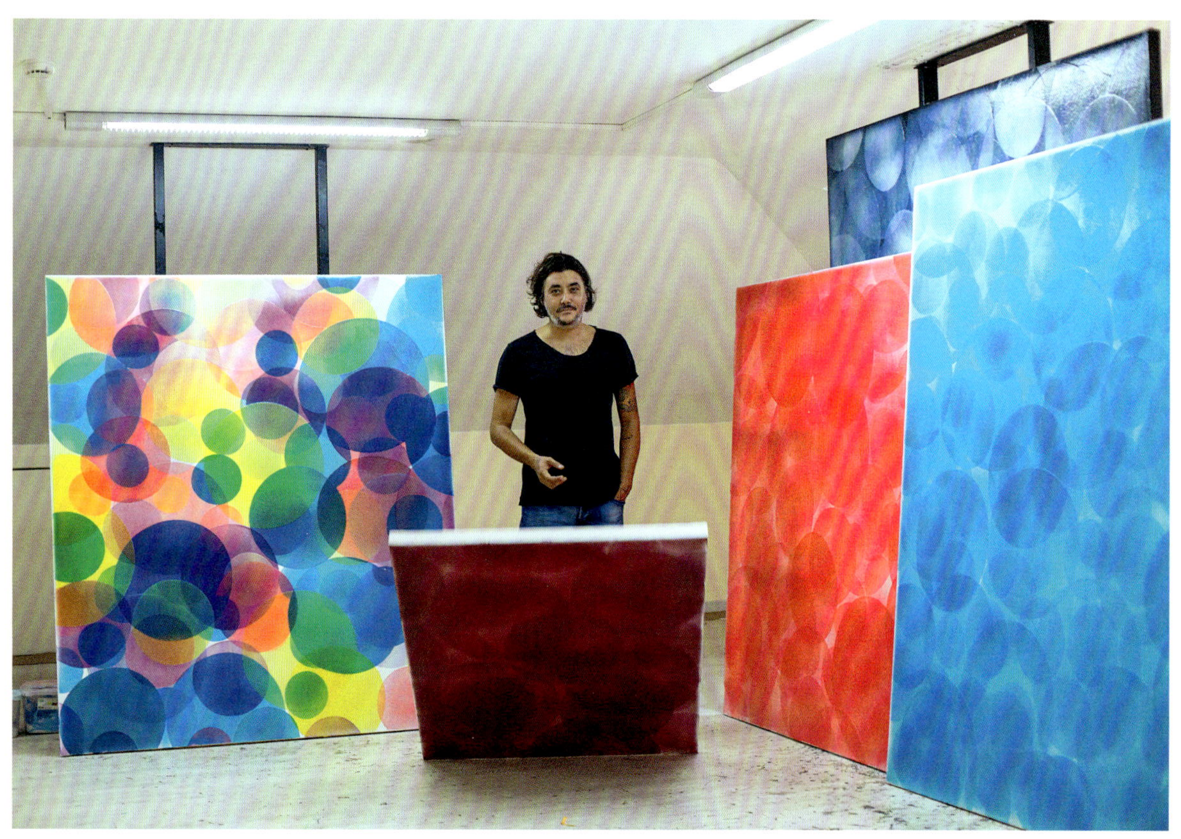

2. Nejat Satı in his studio, Istanbul, 2020
Photo: Nazlı Erdemirel

time phases seem to be connected with each other. On the other hand, Satı refuses to use a method or "mesh" that is too definite, which seems more like an art brand and signature; a dilemma that conceptually involves radical painting, since the frame, as mentioned above, has to be very narrow. Nejat Satı evades this dilemma, since he obviously carries out his work as a comparable experimental test. Sometimes the squeegee allows a more impulsive action. Unlike oil- or water-based paints or expressive color field painting, however, the application of the gel can only cause a sudden solidification of a process. It is inconceivable that something can be corrected. And if a paint application is absolutely unsuccessful, then the entire painting must be produced anew.

With his work, Nejat Satı creates a sovereign position within the contemporary Turkish art scene. With his paintings, he offers us a self-talk with the other. But what is the other? Who is the other when it appears to us from the image like in the mirror as an echo of our other self? A bath in bright colors therefore remains deceptive.

Works

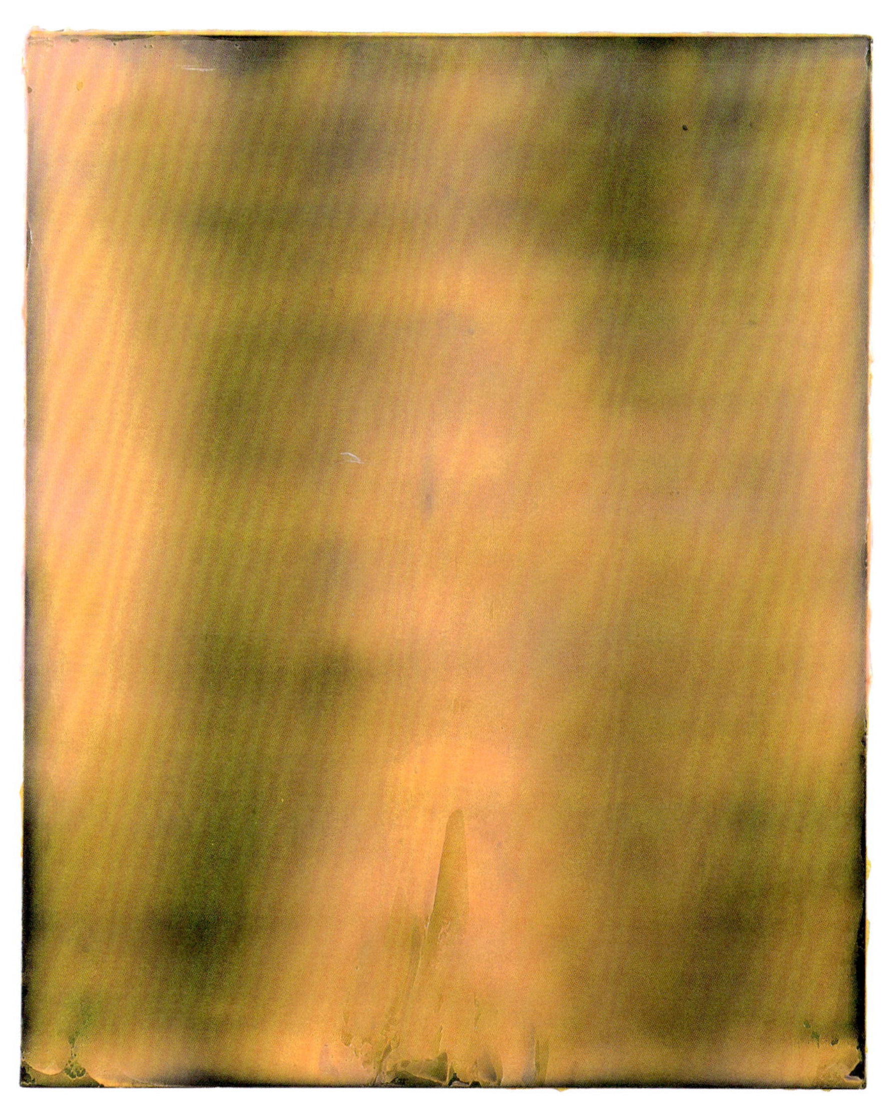

Untitled / Structure series
2013
Acrylic and heavy gel on canvas
130 × 120 cm

Untitled / Structure series
2013
Acrylic and heavy gel on canvas
160 × 110 cm

Blue Structure
2014
Acrylic and heavy gel on canvas
150 × 120 cm

Following pages

Untitled / Structure series
2014
Acrylic and heavy gel on canvas
Diptych, 230 × 170 cm each

Structure 88 / Structure series
2014
Acrylic and heavy gel on canvas
140 × 100 cm

Black Structure 7 / Structure series
2015
Acrylic and heavy gel on canvas
110 × 80 cm

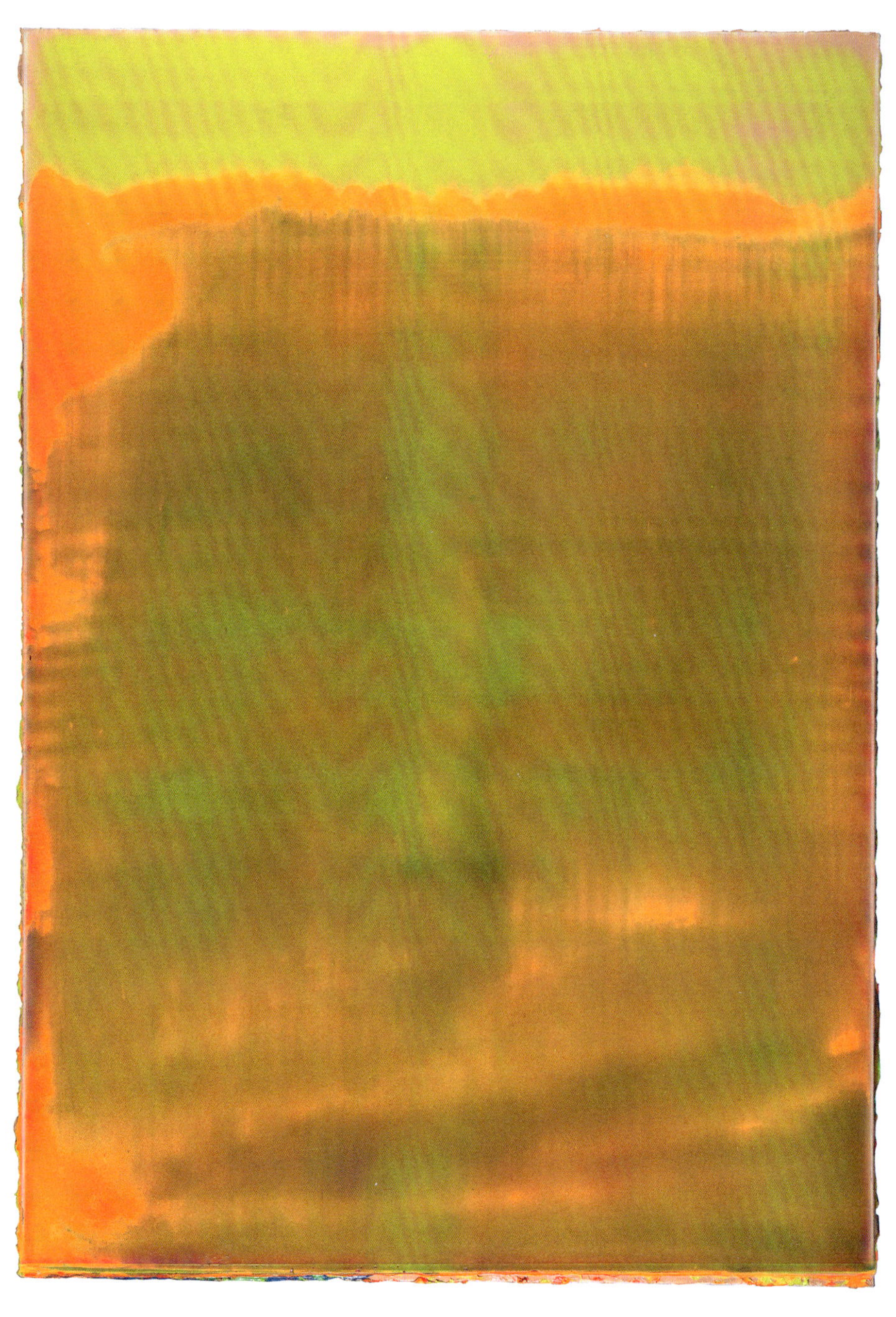

Structure 67 / *Structure* series
2015
Acrylic and heavy gel on canvas
170 × 120 cm

Black Structure 6 / Structure series
2015
Acrylic and heavy gel on canvas
110 × 80 cm

Untitled / *Structure* series
2016
Acrylic and heavy gel on canvas
120 × 70 cm

Rainbow / Structure series
2016
Acrylic and heavy gel on canvas
60 × 50 cm

Rainbow / Structure series
2016
Acrylic and heavy gel on canvas
60 × 50 cm

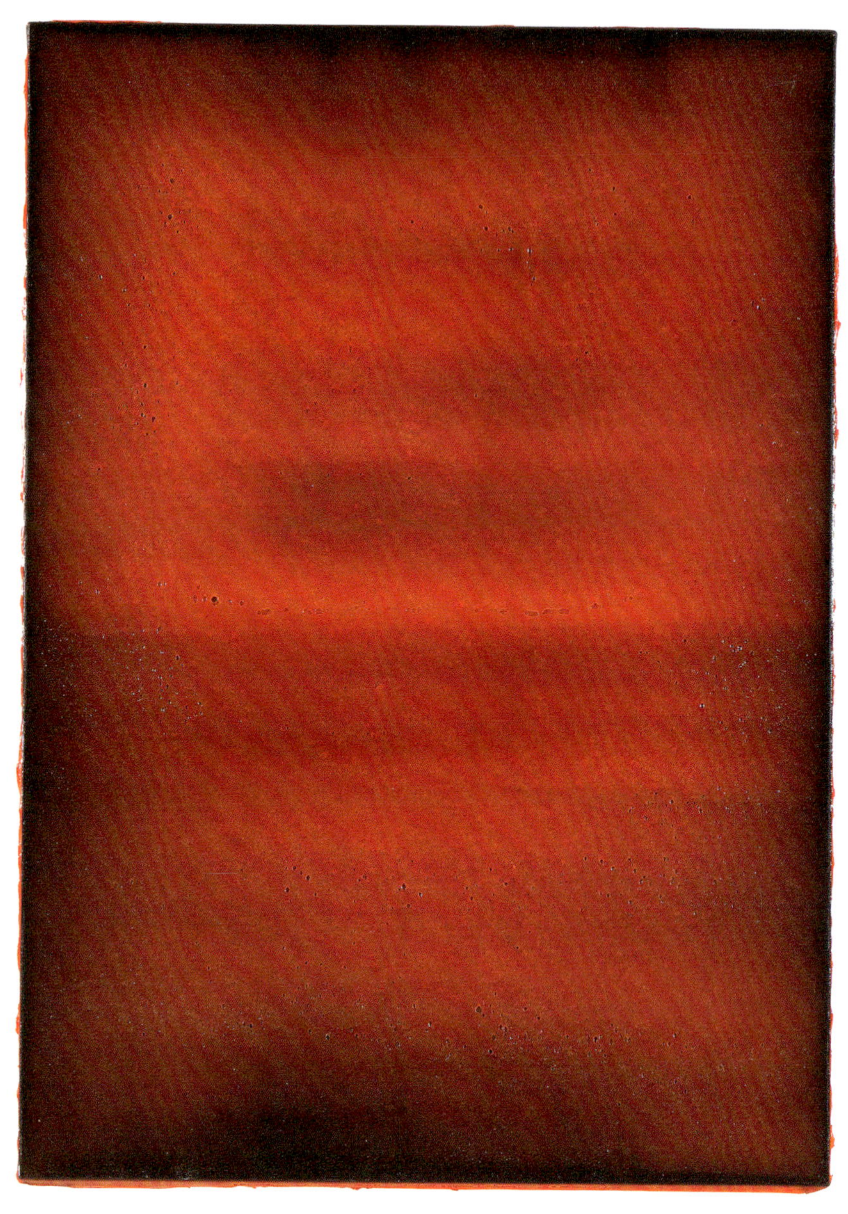

Red and Black / Structure series
2017
Acrylic and heavy gel on canvas
100 × 72 cm

Aurora / Structure series
2017
Acrylic and heavy gel on canvas
80 × 60 cm

Dark Psy / Structure series
2018
Acrylic and heavy gel on canvas
150 × 100 cm

Dark Psy / Structure series
2018
Acrylic and heavy gel on canvas
150 × 100 cm

Untitled / Structure series
2018
Acrylic and heavy gel on canvas
150 × 120 cm

Untitled / Structure series
2019
Acrylic and heavy gel on canvas
123 × 89 cm

Untitled / Structure series
2019
Acrylic and heavy gel on canvas
123 × 89 cm

Untitled / Structure series
2019
Acrylic and heavy gel on canvas
103 × 88 cm

Untitled / Structure series
2021
Acrylic and heavy gel on canvas
80 × 60 cm

Untitled / Structure series
2021
Acrylic and heavy gel on canvas
80 × 60 cm

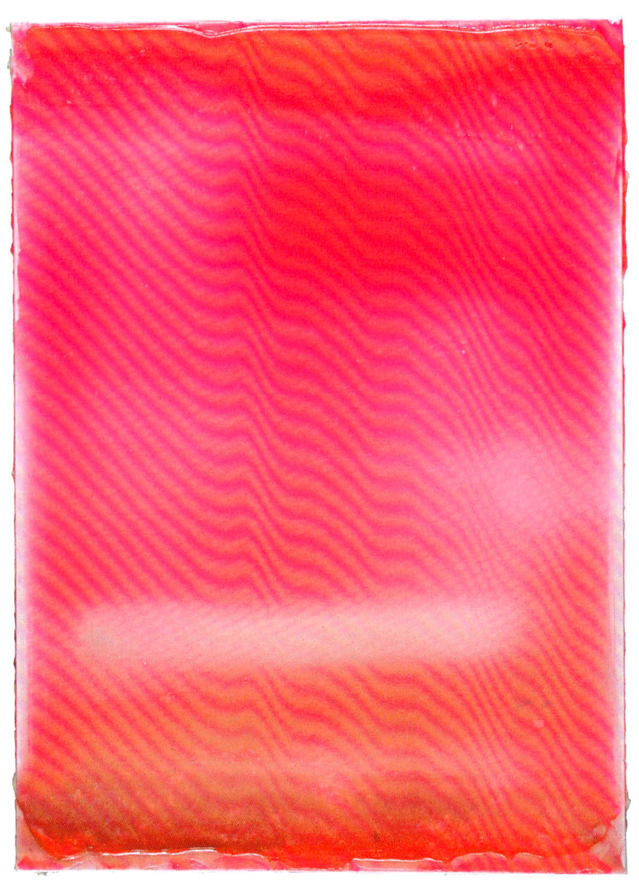

Untitled / *Structure* series
2021
Acrylic and heavy gel on canvas
80 × 60 cm

Untitled / Structure series
2021
Acrylic and heavy gel on canvas
80 × 60 cm

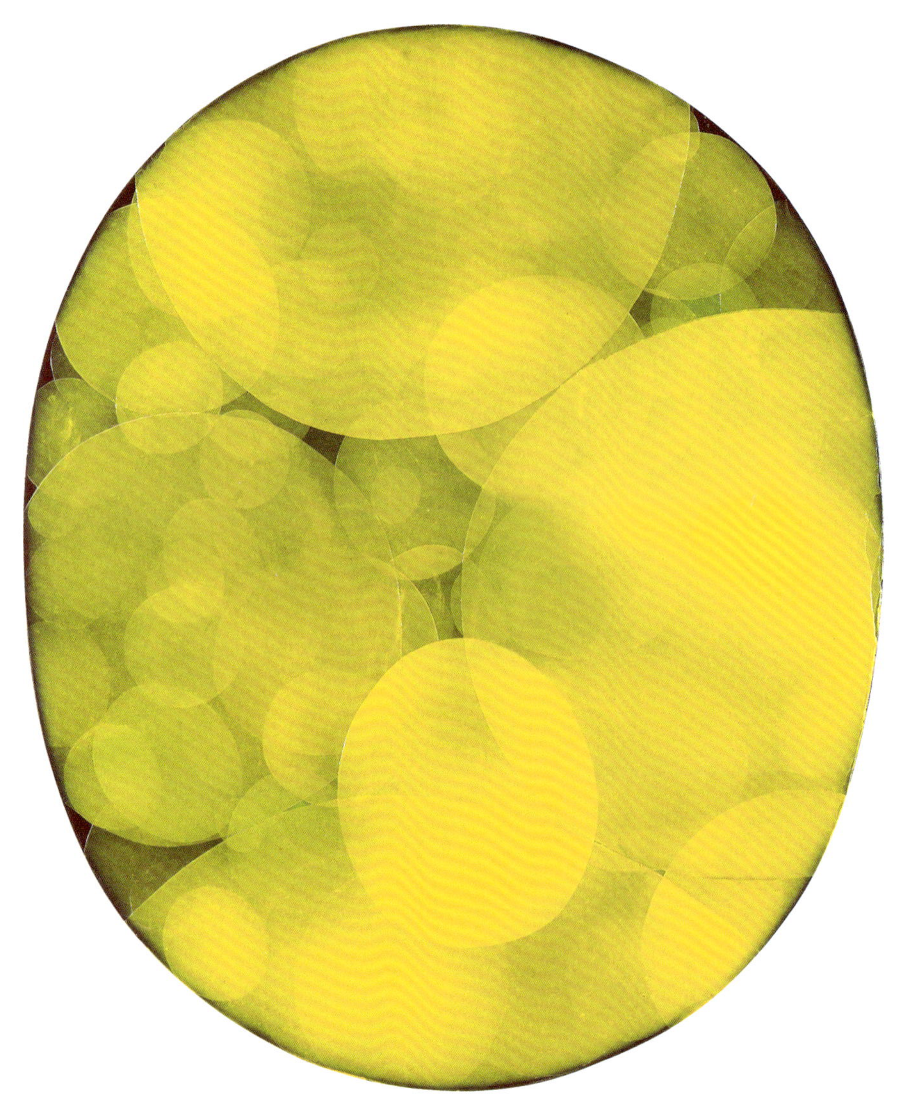

Bad Piece / Organic series
2011
Acrylic and heavy gel on canvas
120 × 90 cm

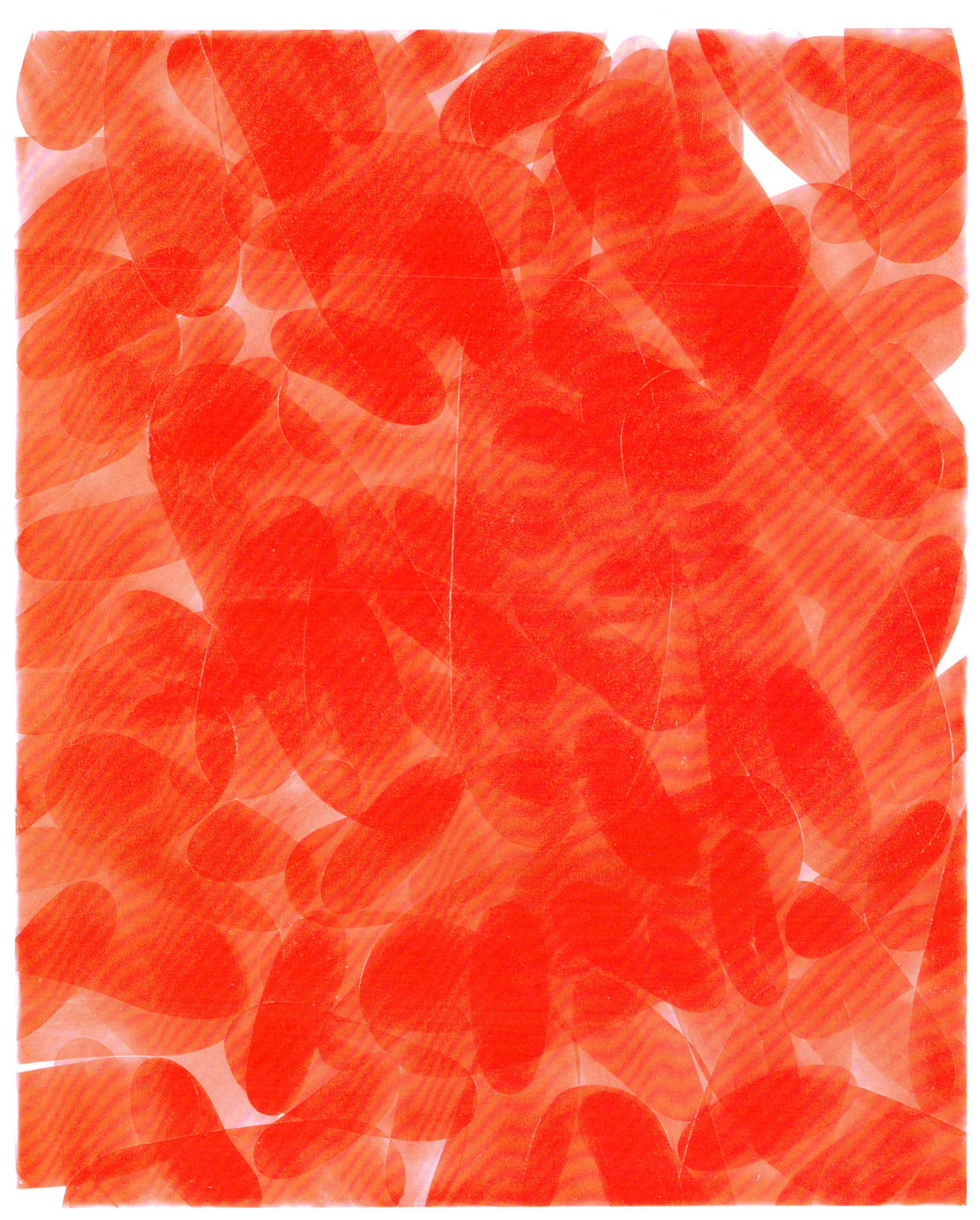

Hemoglobin / Organic series
2012
Acrylic and heavy gel on canvas
160 × 150 cm

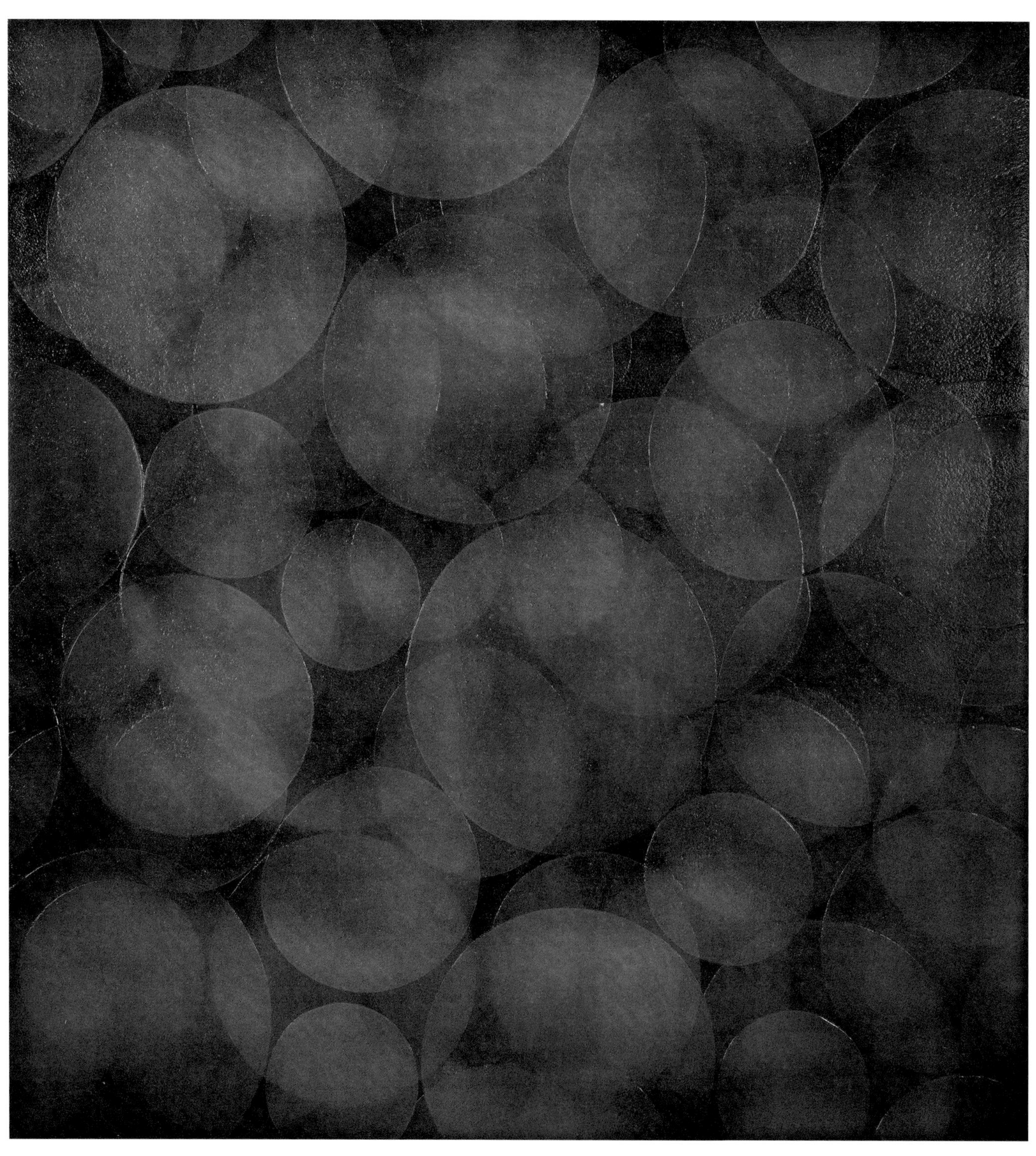

Organic Abstract IB-701
2020
Acrylic and heavy gel on canvas
200 × 190 cm

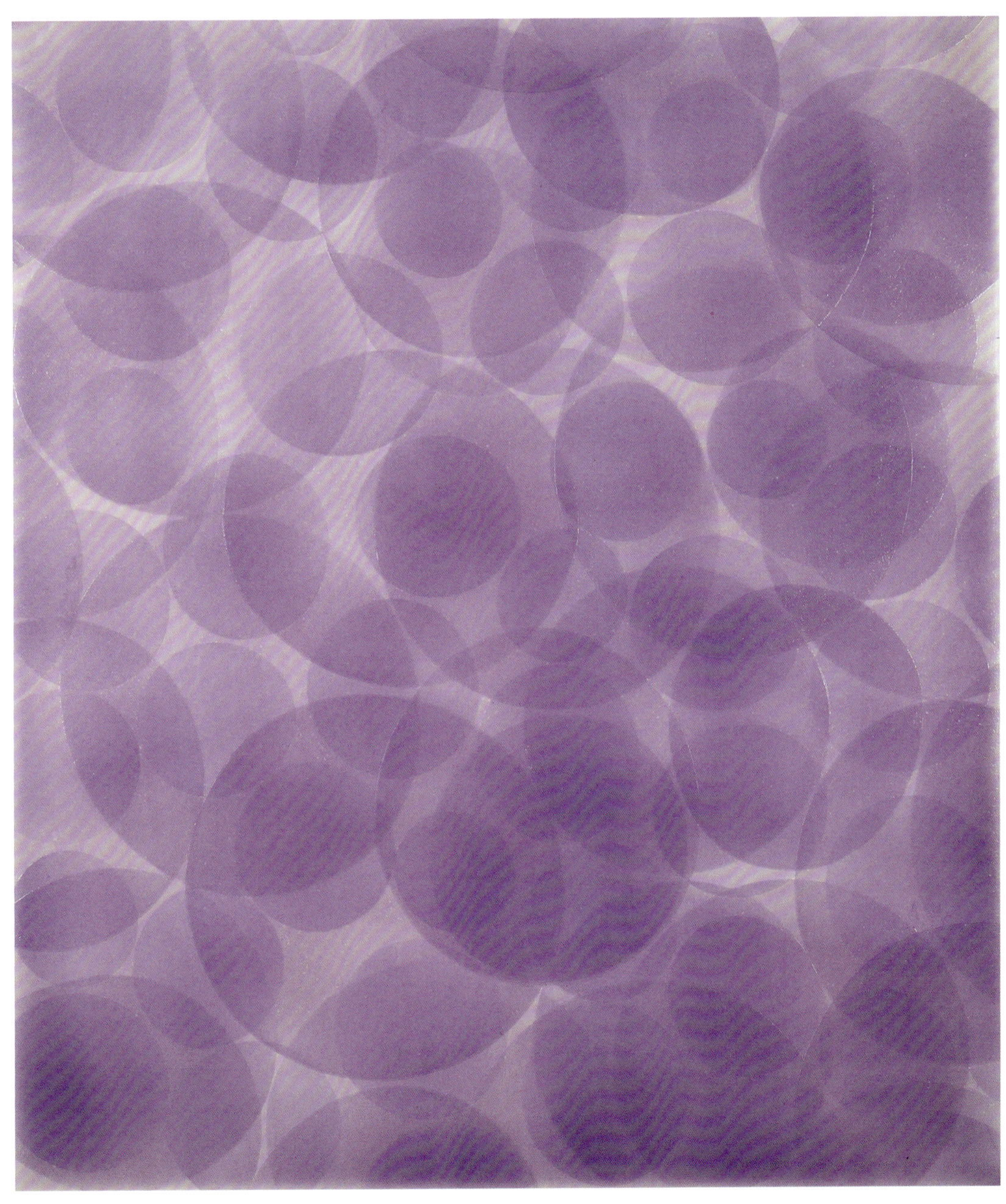

Following pages

SH-1467 / Organic series
2020
Acrylic and heavy gel on canvas
150 × 130 cm

TDM-317 / Organic series
2020
Acrylic and heavy gel on canvas
170 × 300 cm

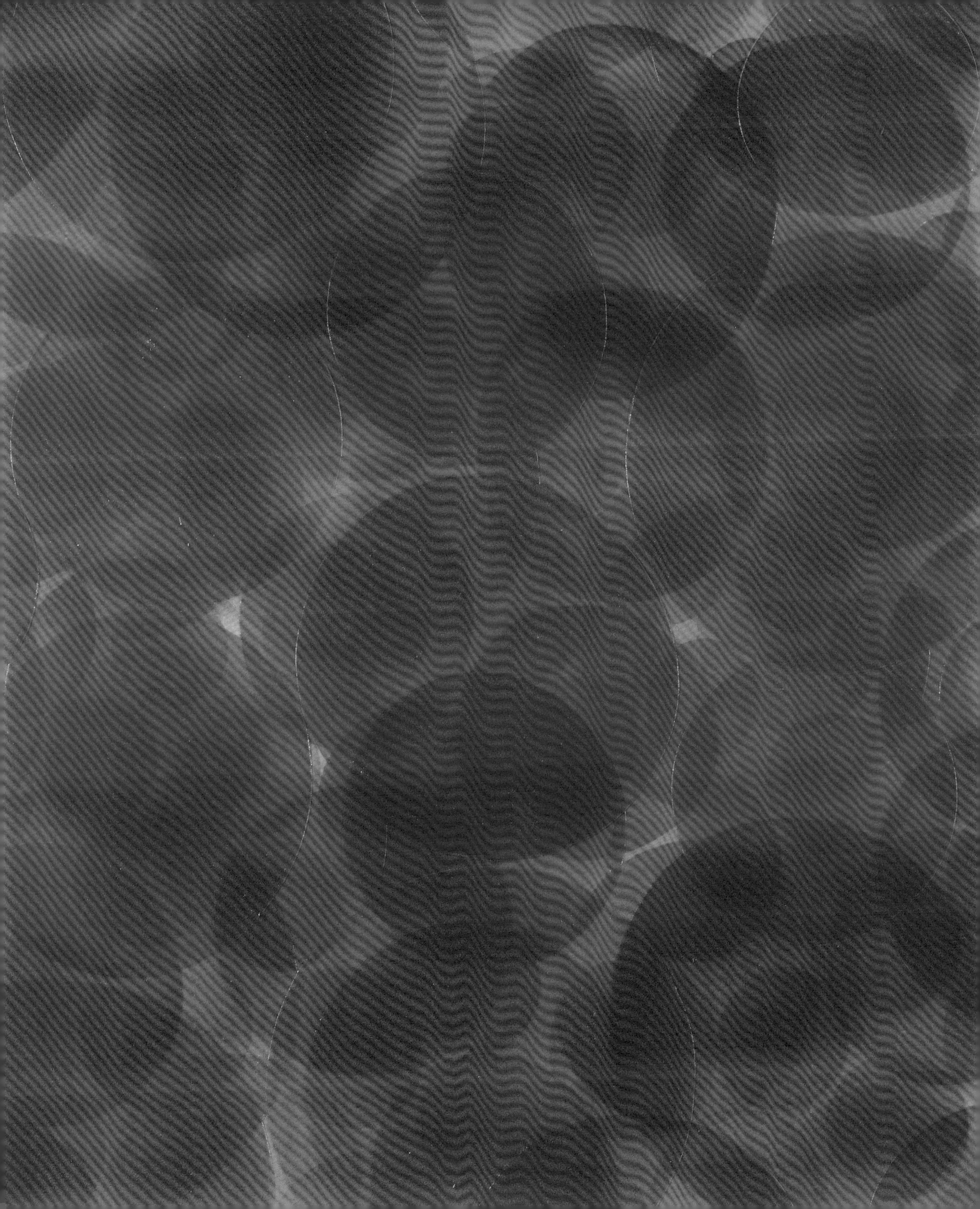

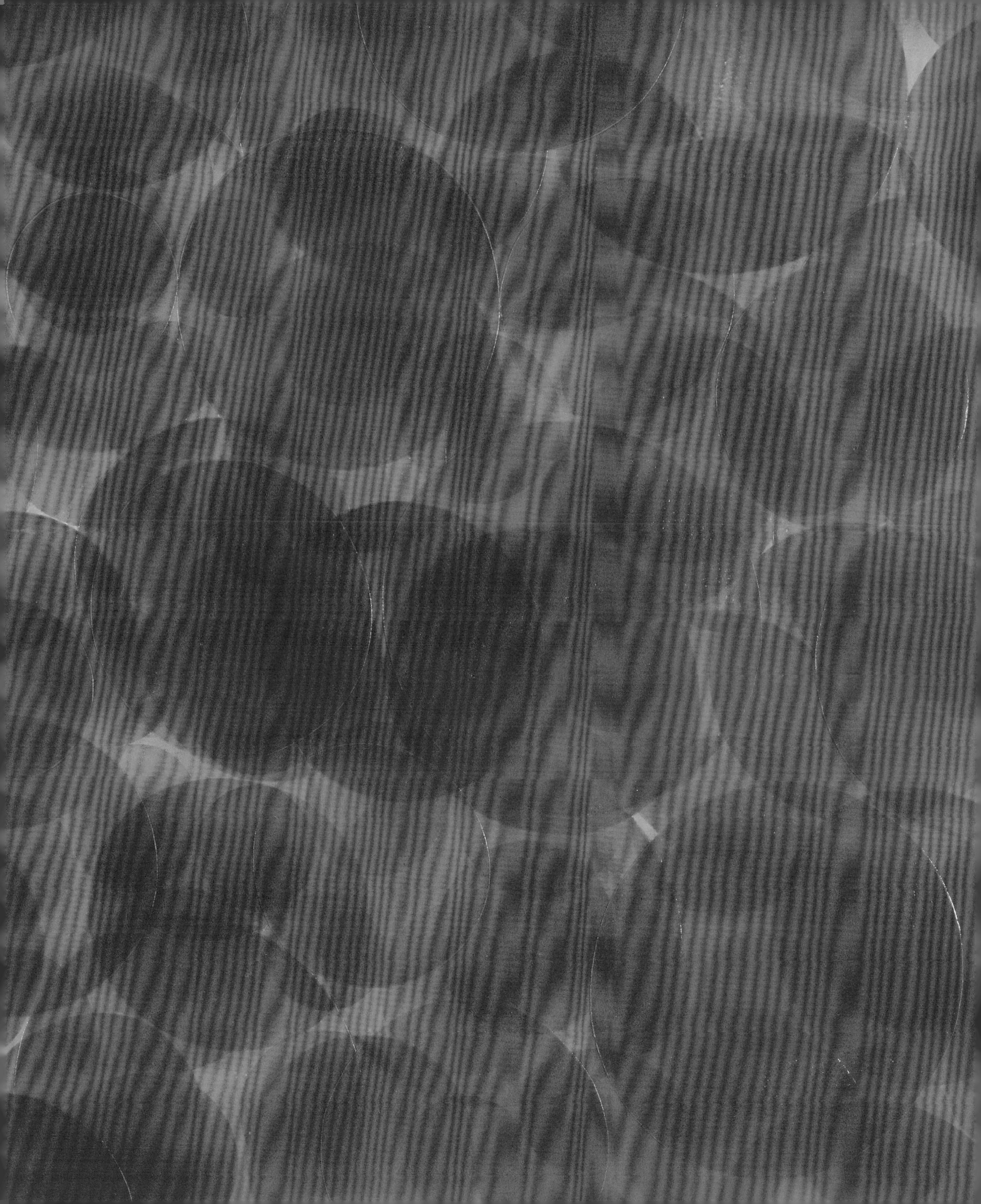

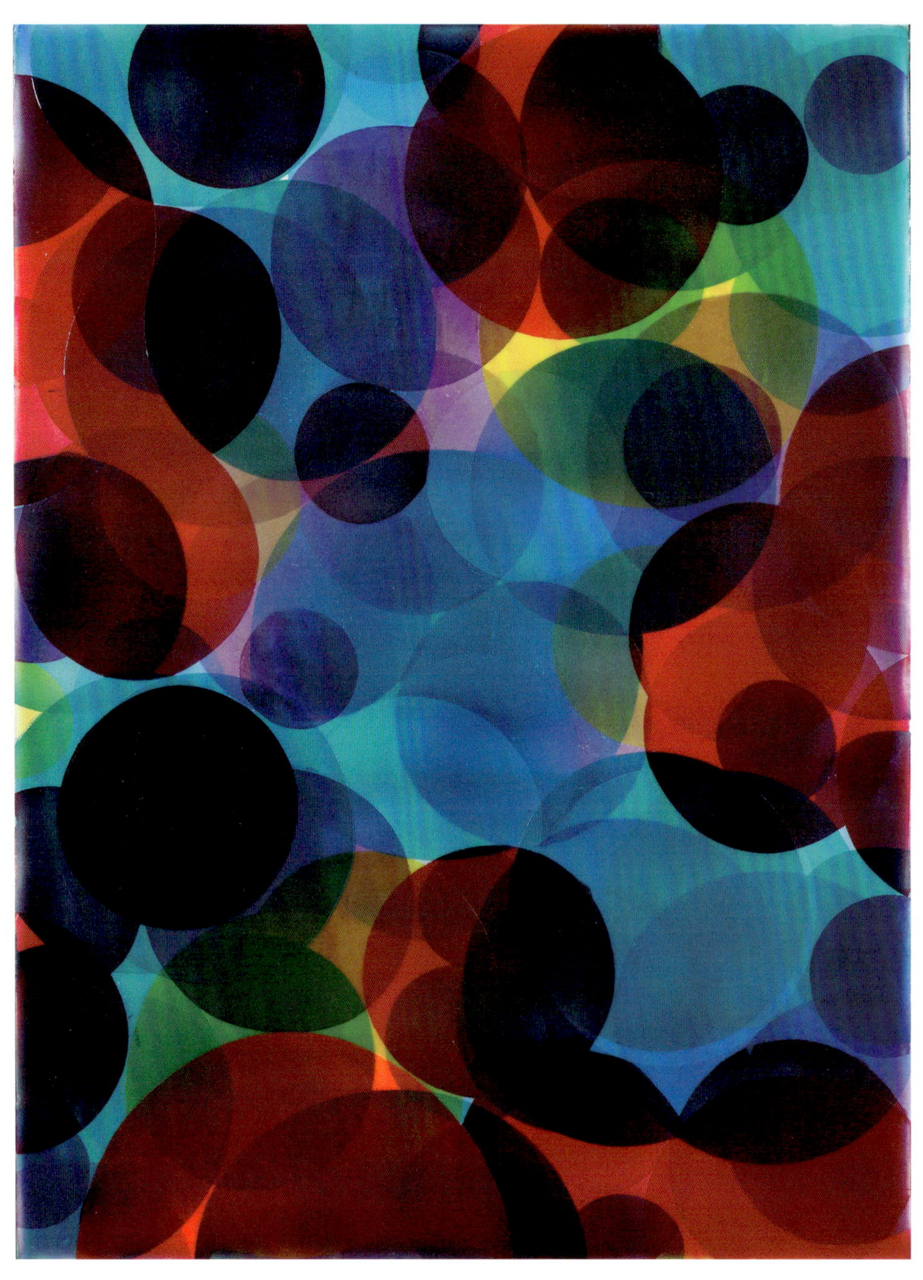

Untitled / Organic series
2021
Acrylic and heavy gel on canvas
150 × 110 cm

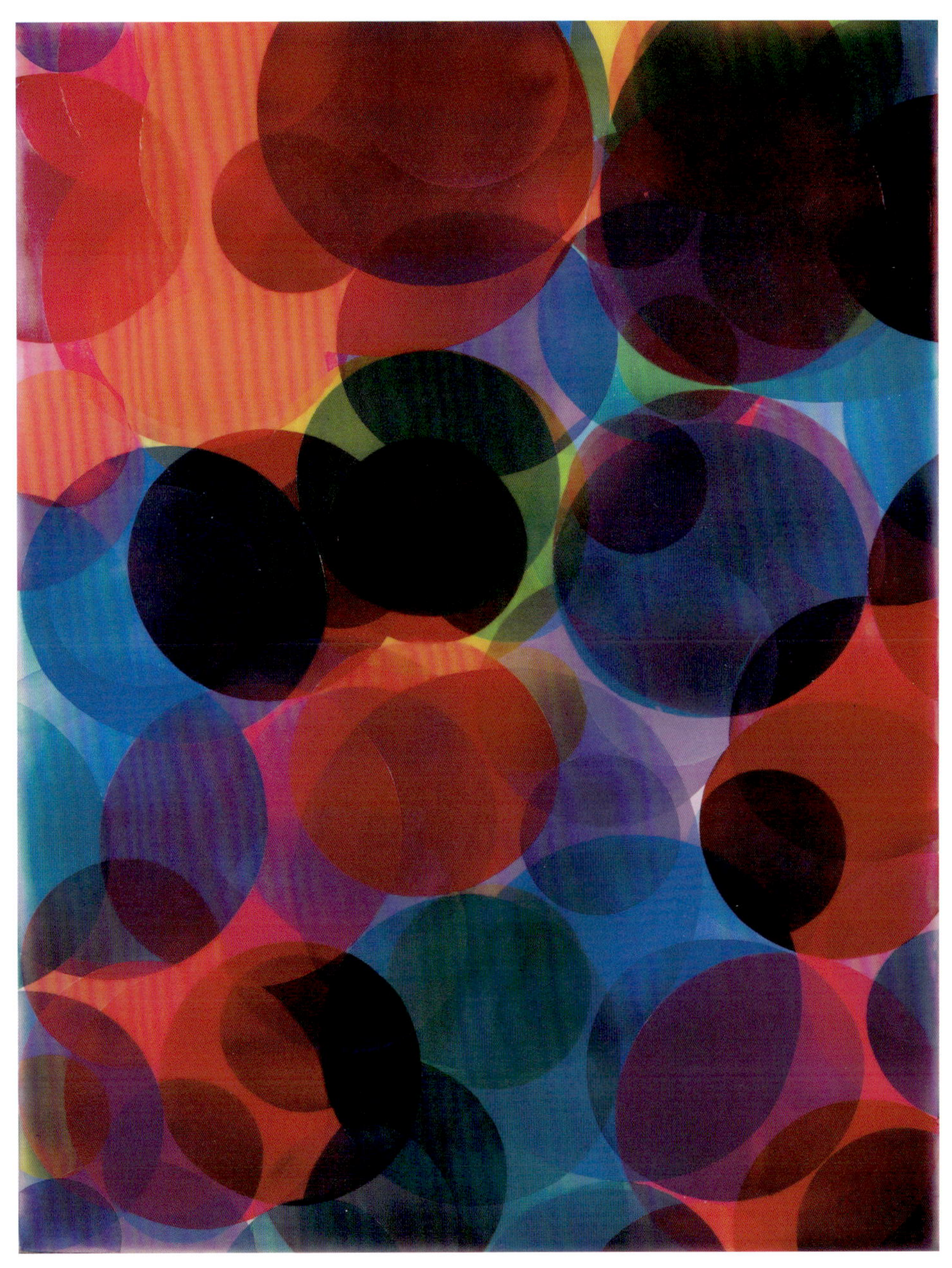

Untitled / Organic series
2021
Acrylic and heavy gel on canvas
150 × 110 cm

PY-3 / Organic series
2020
Acrylic and heavy gel on canvas
180 × 160 cm

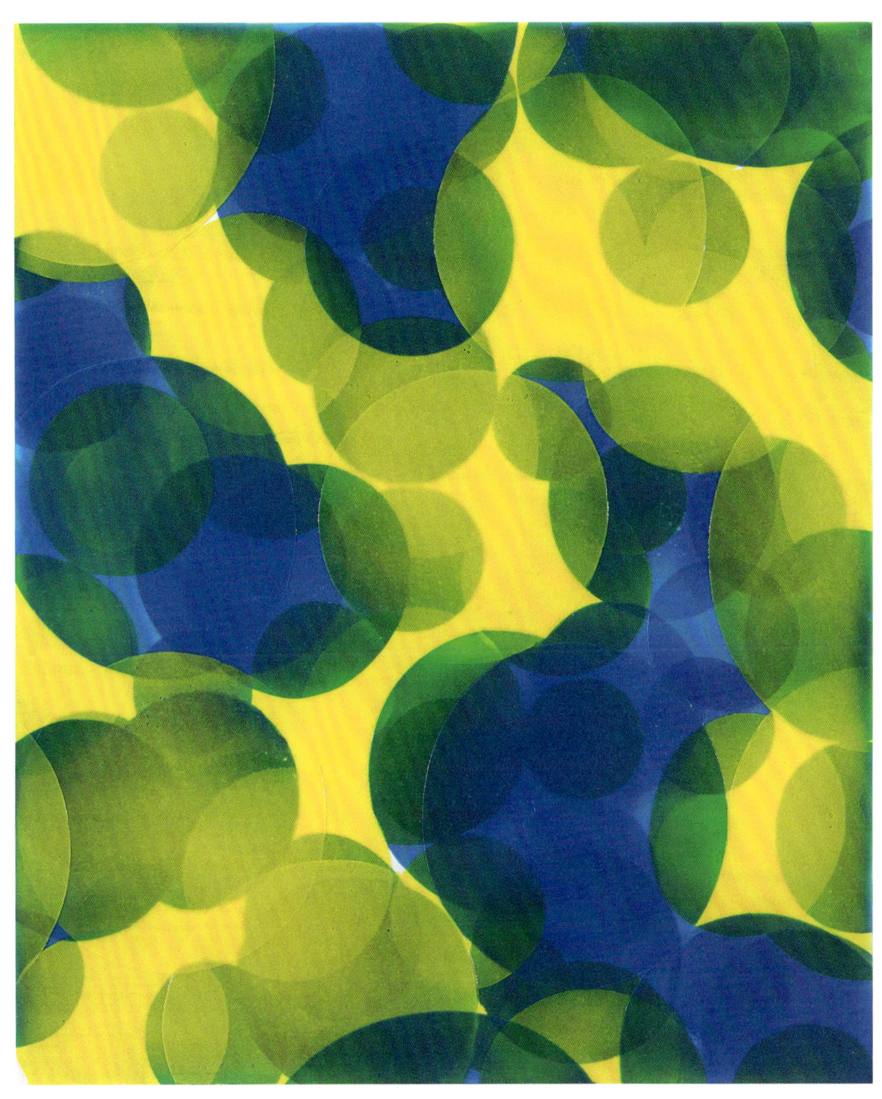

FB-1907 / Organic series
2020
Acrylic and heavy gel on canvas
120 × 100 cm

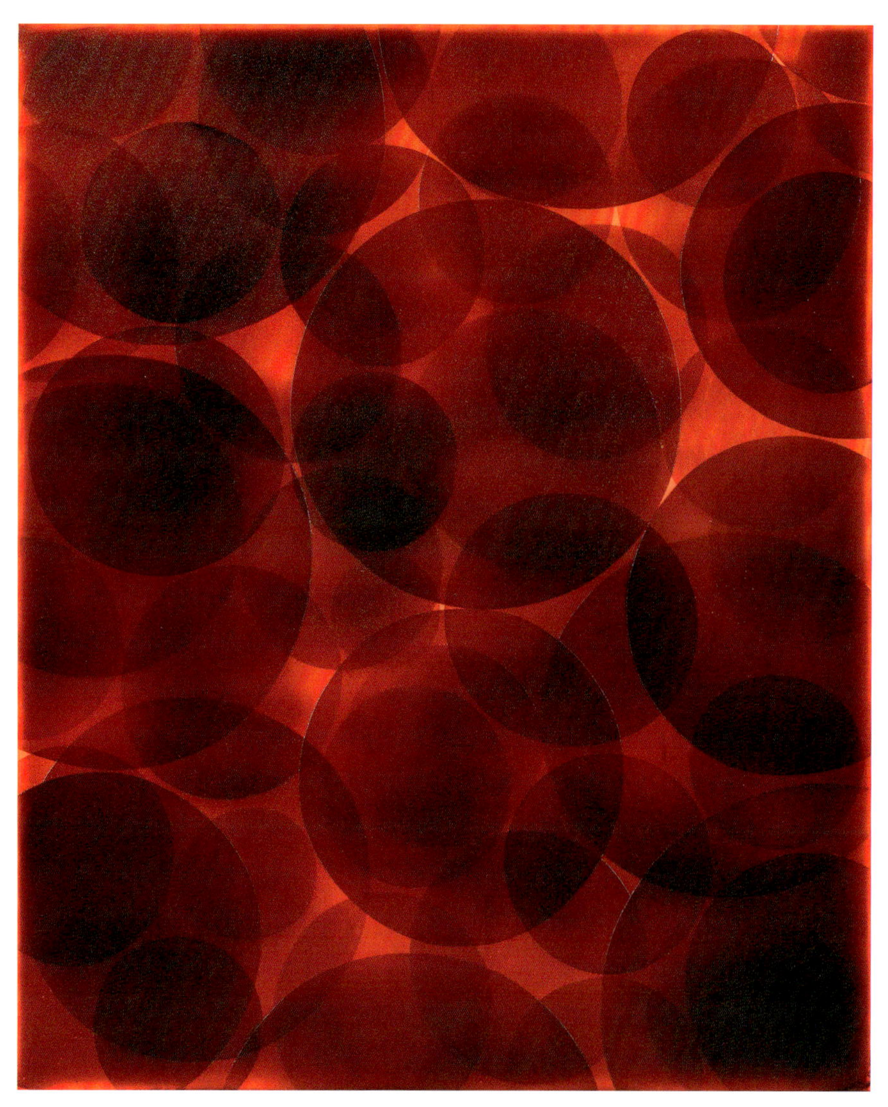

RGB-4 / Organic series
2021
Acrylic and heavy gel on canvas
120 × 100 cm

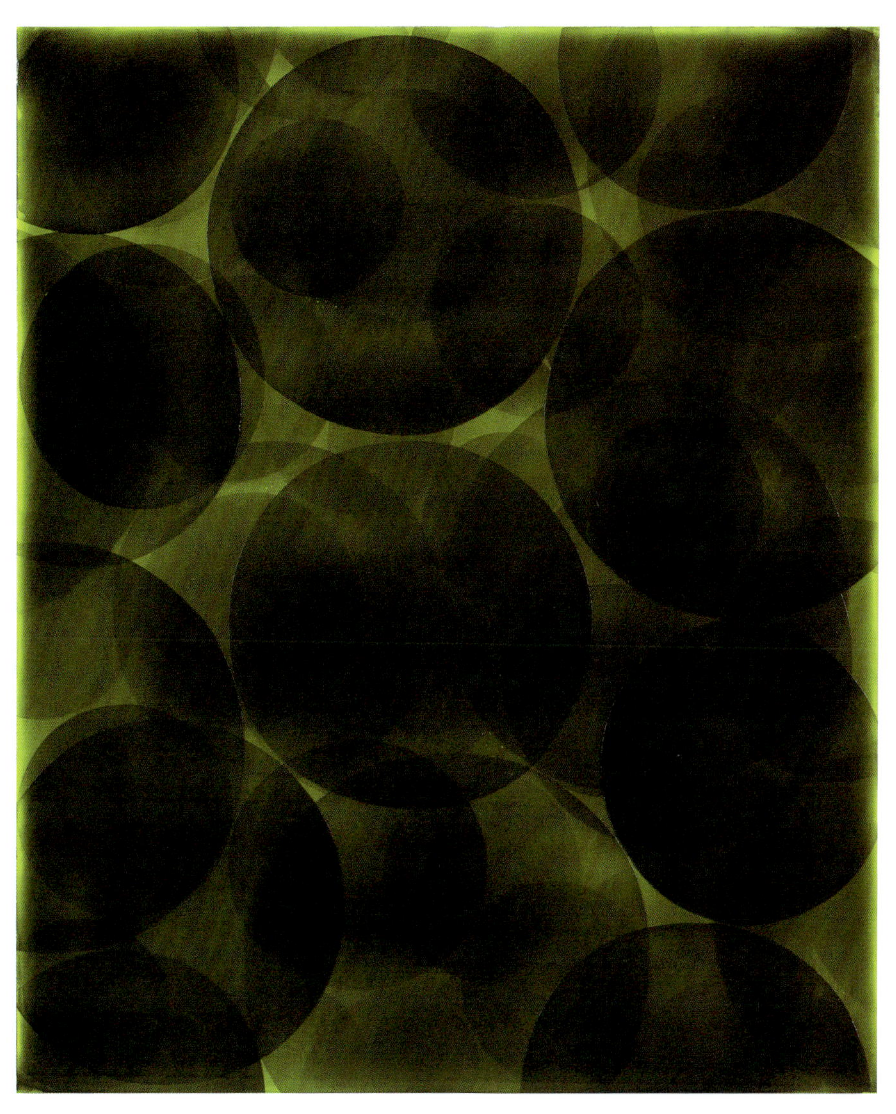

RGB / Organic series
2021
Acrylic and heavy gel on canvas
120 × 100 cm

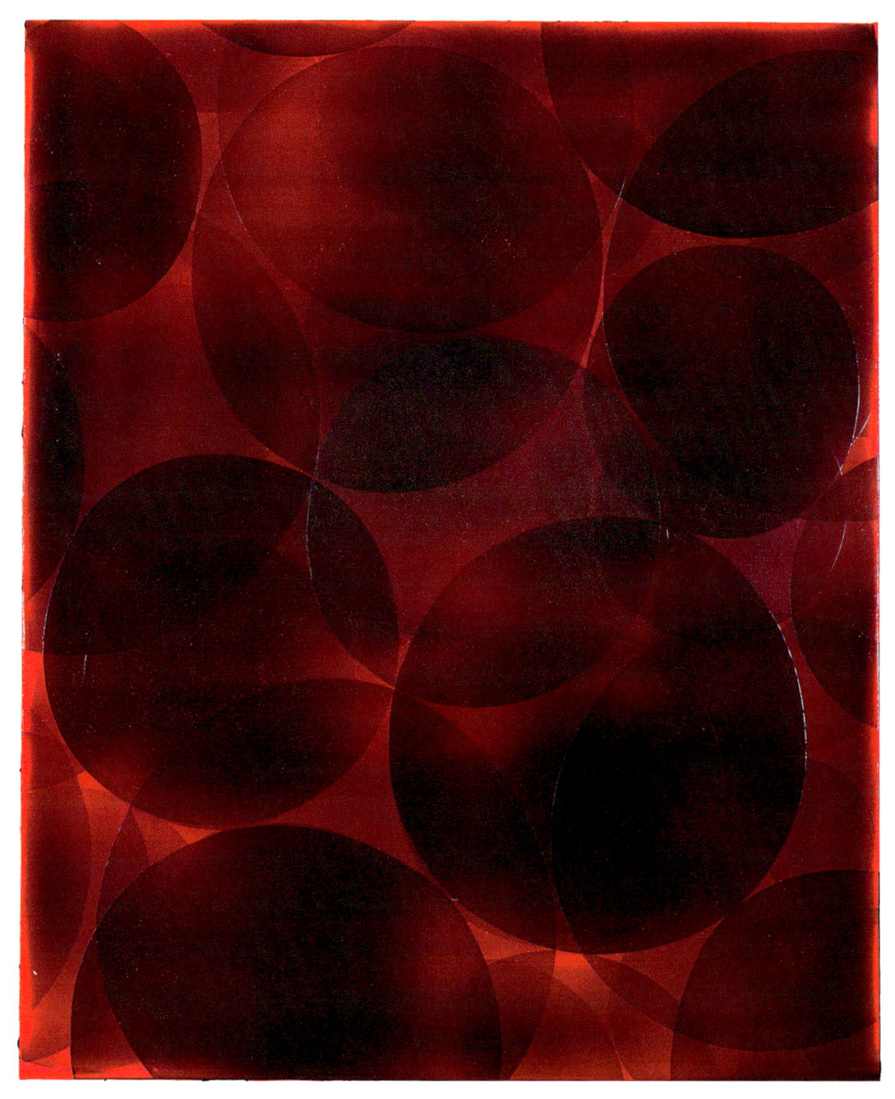

RGB / Organic series
2021
Acrylic and heavy gel on canvas
120 × 100 cm

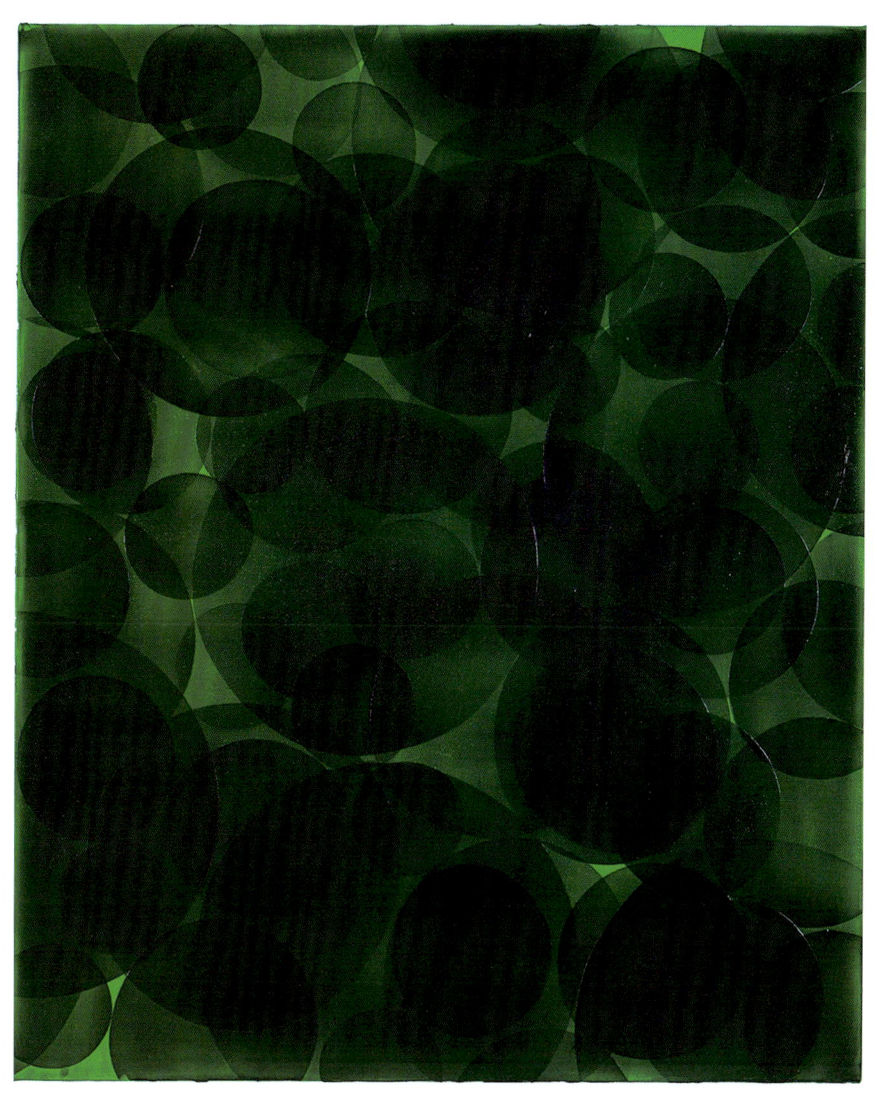

RGB / Organic series
2021
Acrylic and heavy gel on canvas
120 × 100 cm

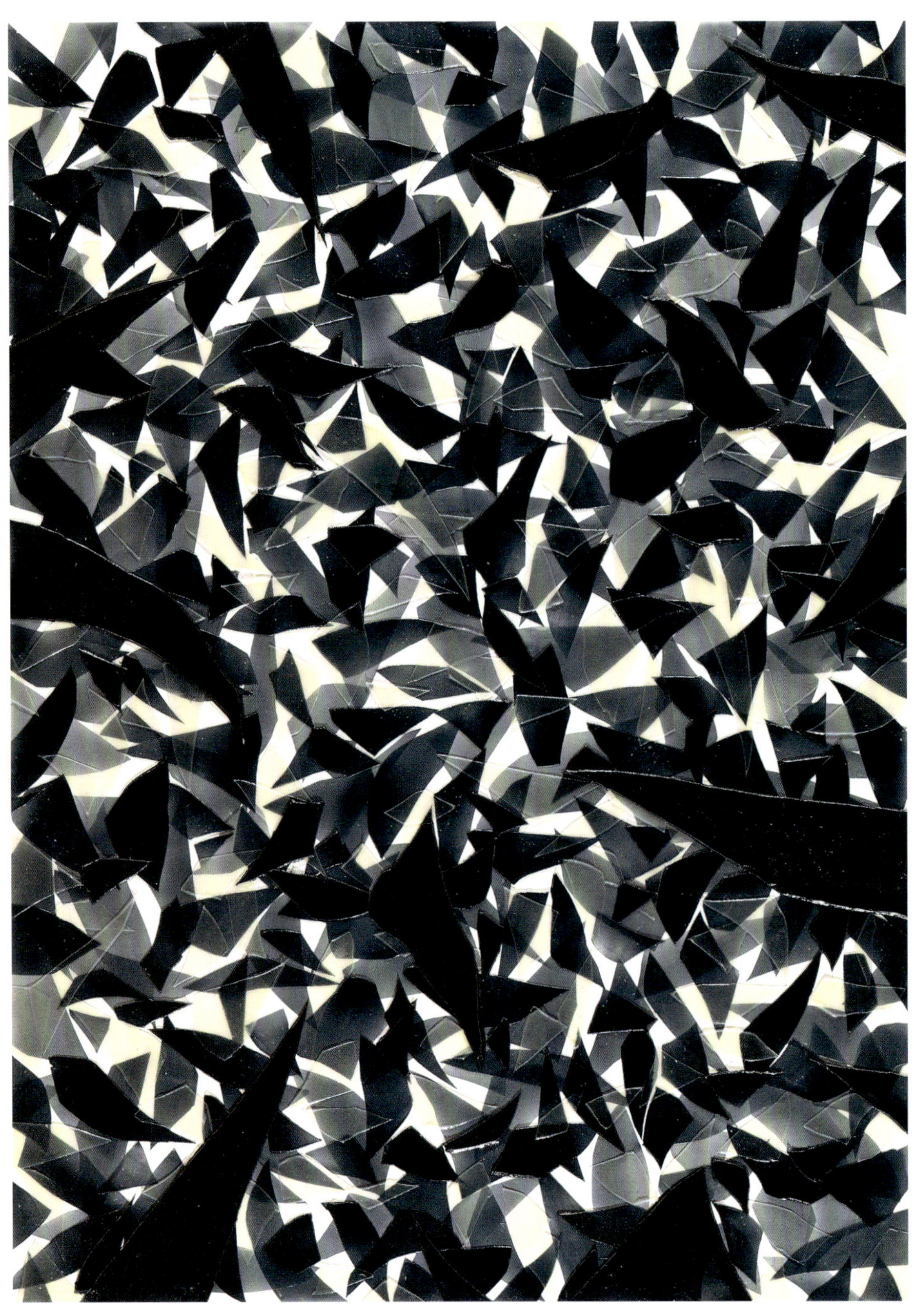

Untitled / Melancholia series
2014
Acrylic and heavy gel on canvas
180 × 130 cm

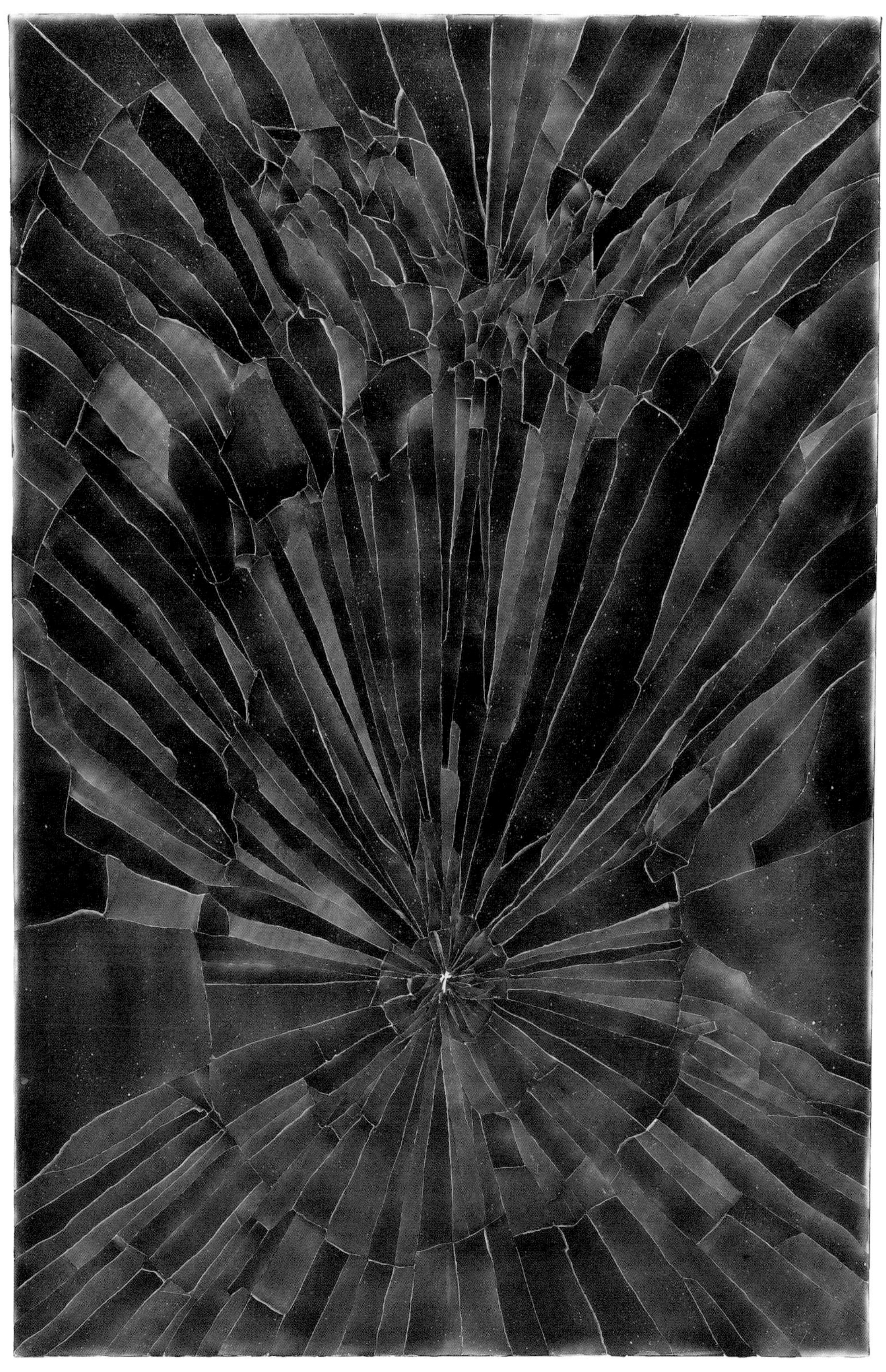

Untitled / *Melancholia* series
2013
Acrylic and heavy gel on canvas
220 × 150 cm

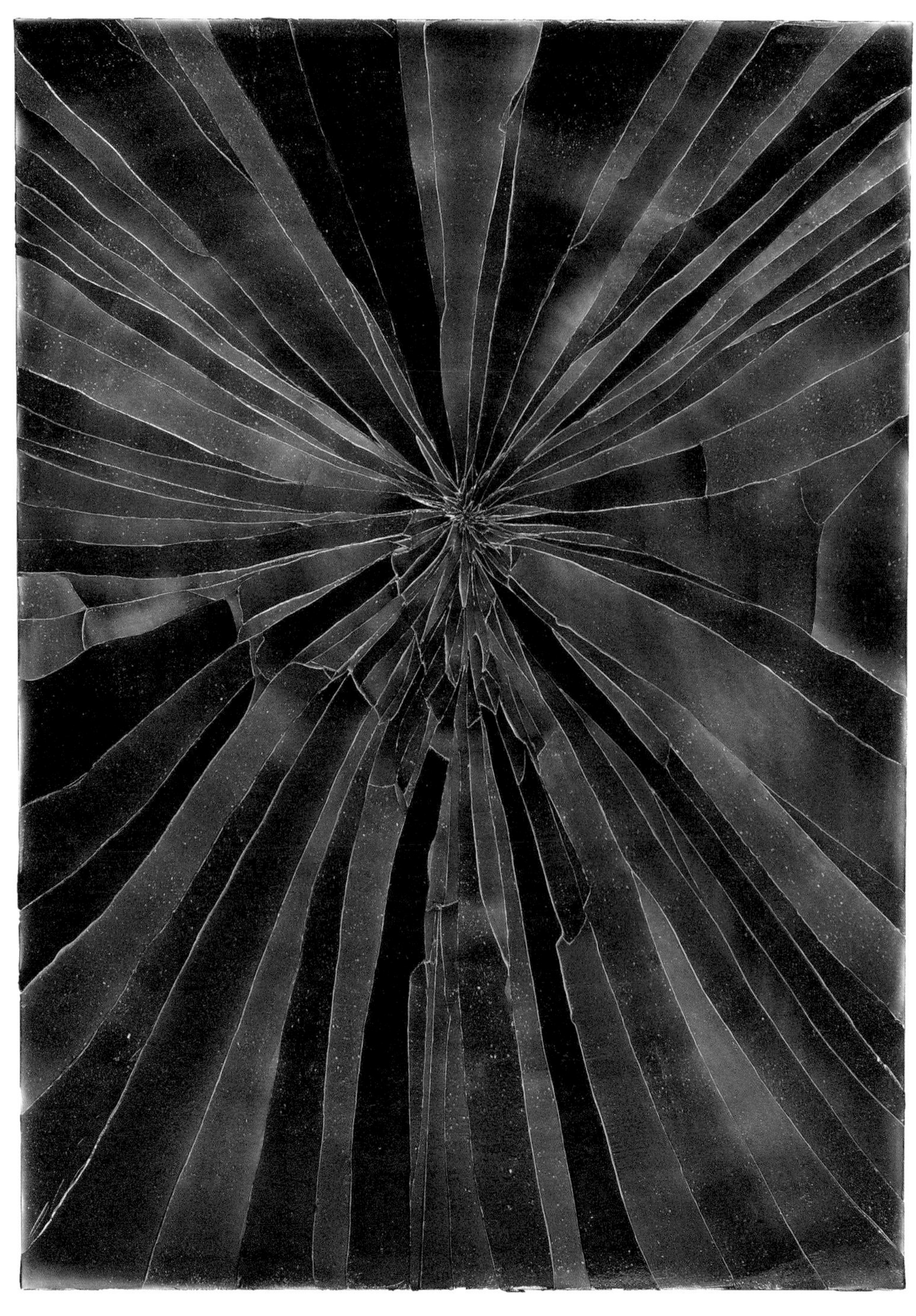

Untitled / Melancholia series
2013
Acrylic and heavy gel on canvas
180 × 130 cm

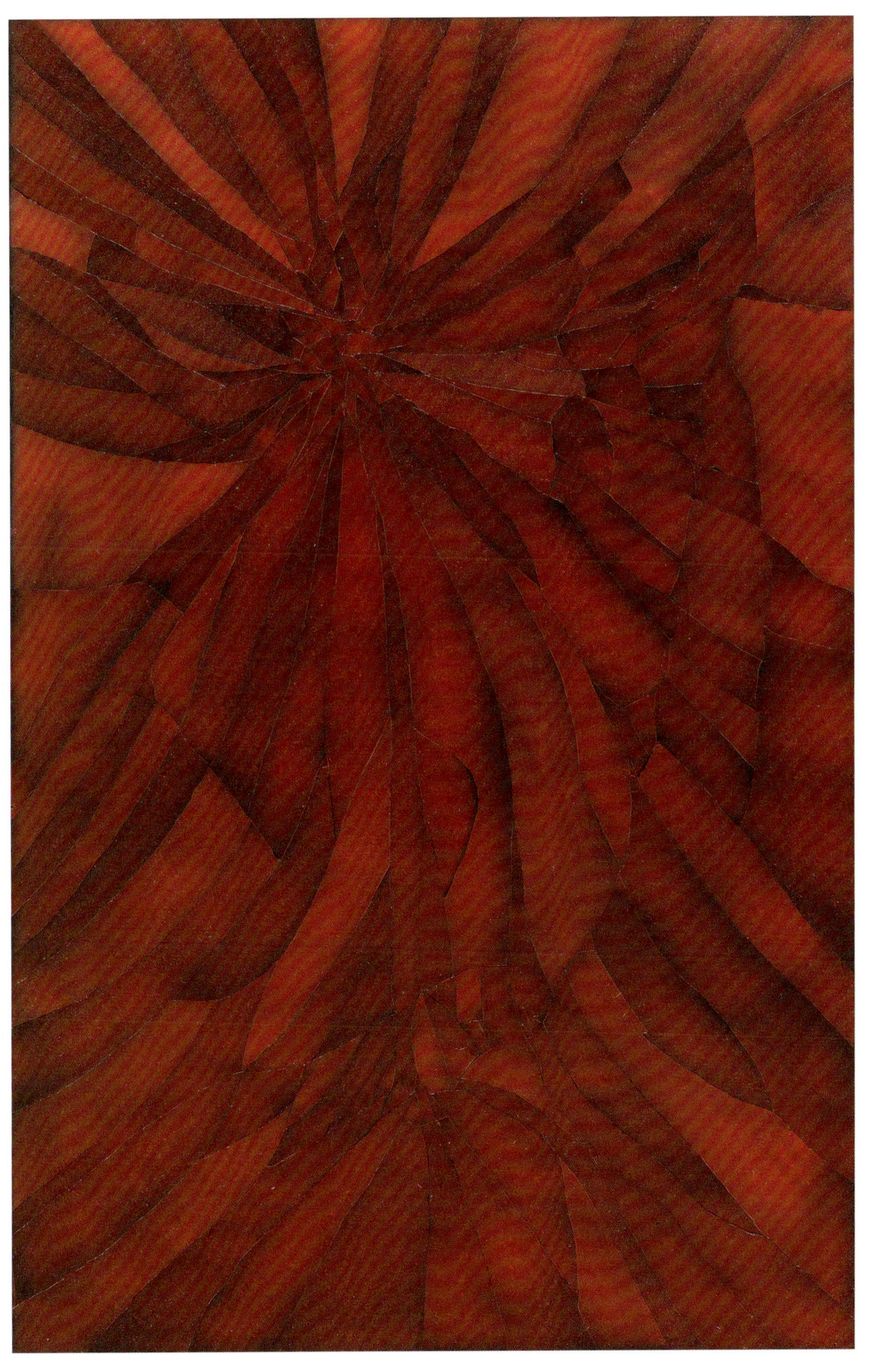

Untitled / Melancholia series
2014
Acrylic and heavy gel on canvas
220 × 140 cm

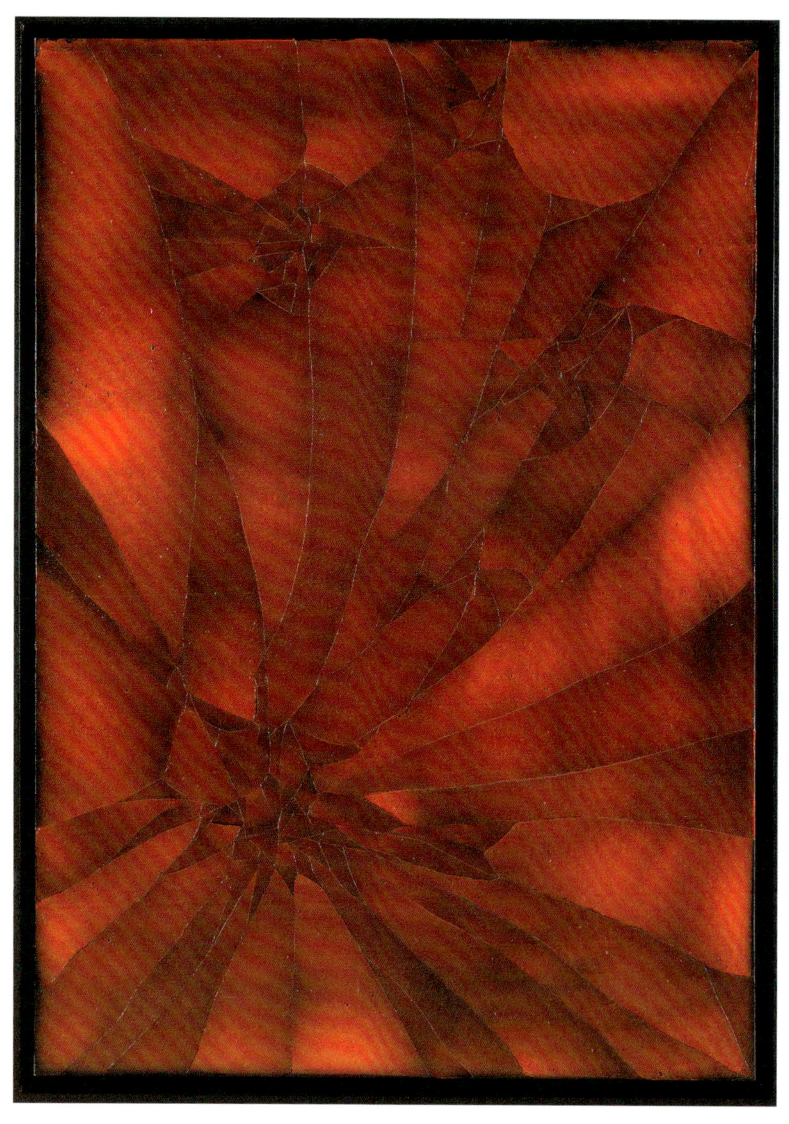

Untitled / Melancholia series
2015
Acrylic and heavy gel on canvas
140 × 100 cm

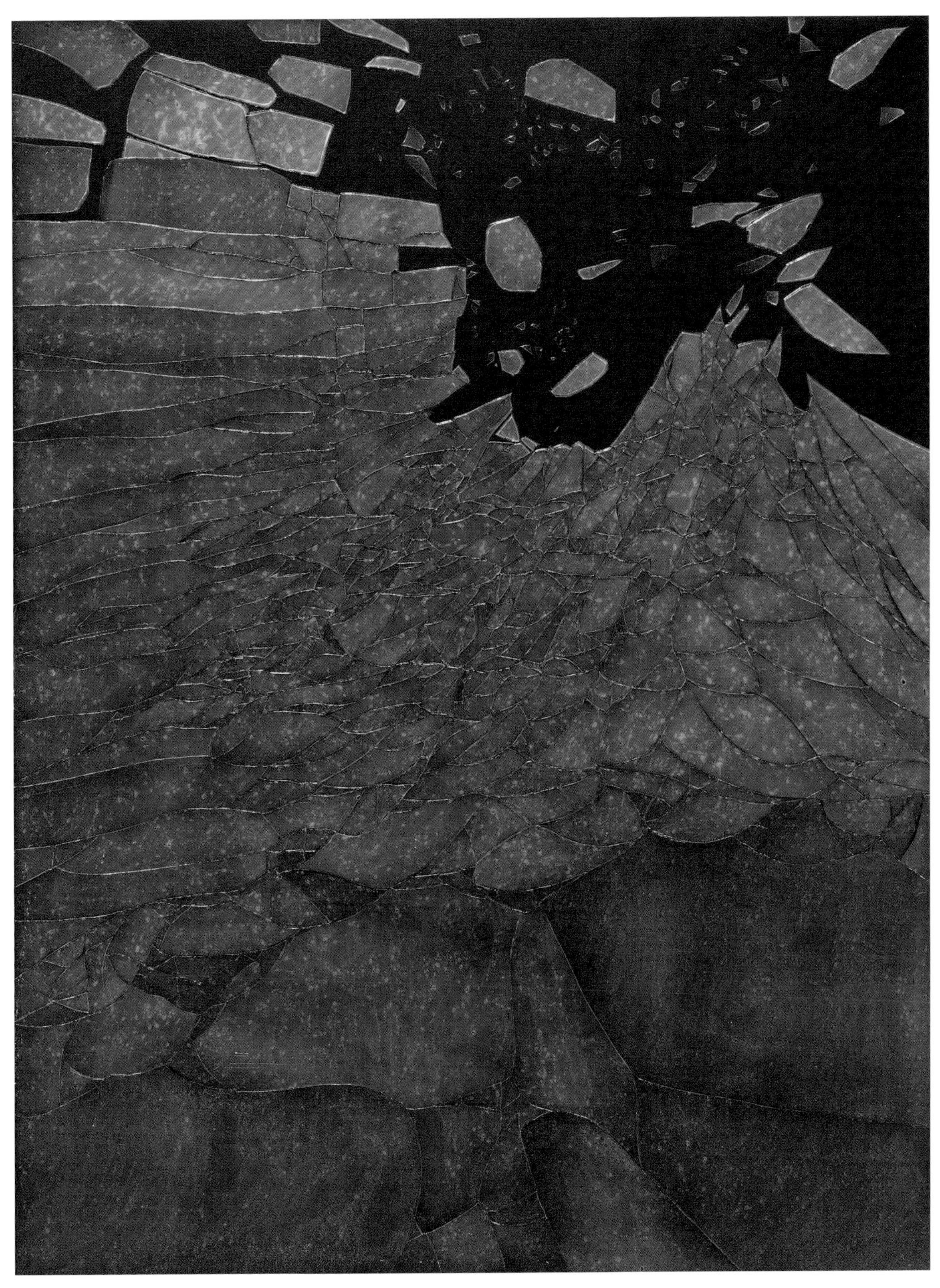

Cracks / Melancholia series
2017
Acrylic and heavy gel on canvas
200 × 150 cm

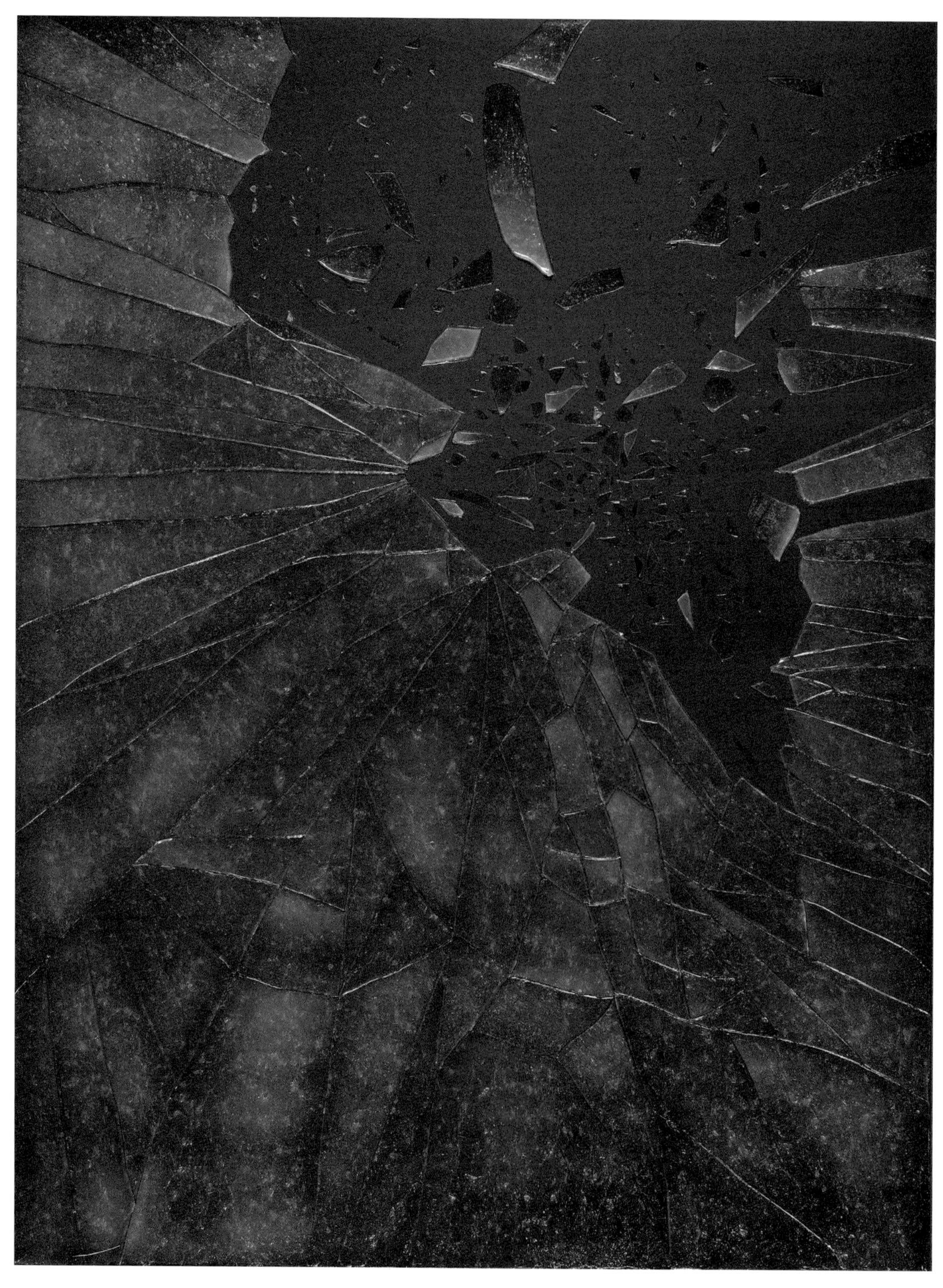

Untitled / *Melancholia* series
2019
Acrylic and heavy gel on canvas
210 × 155 cm

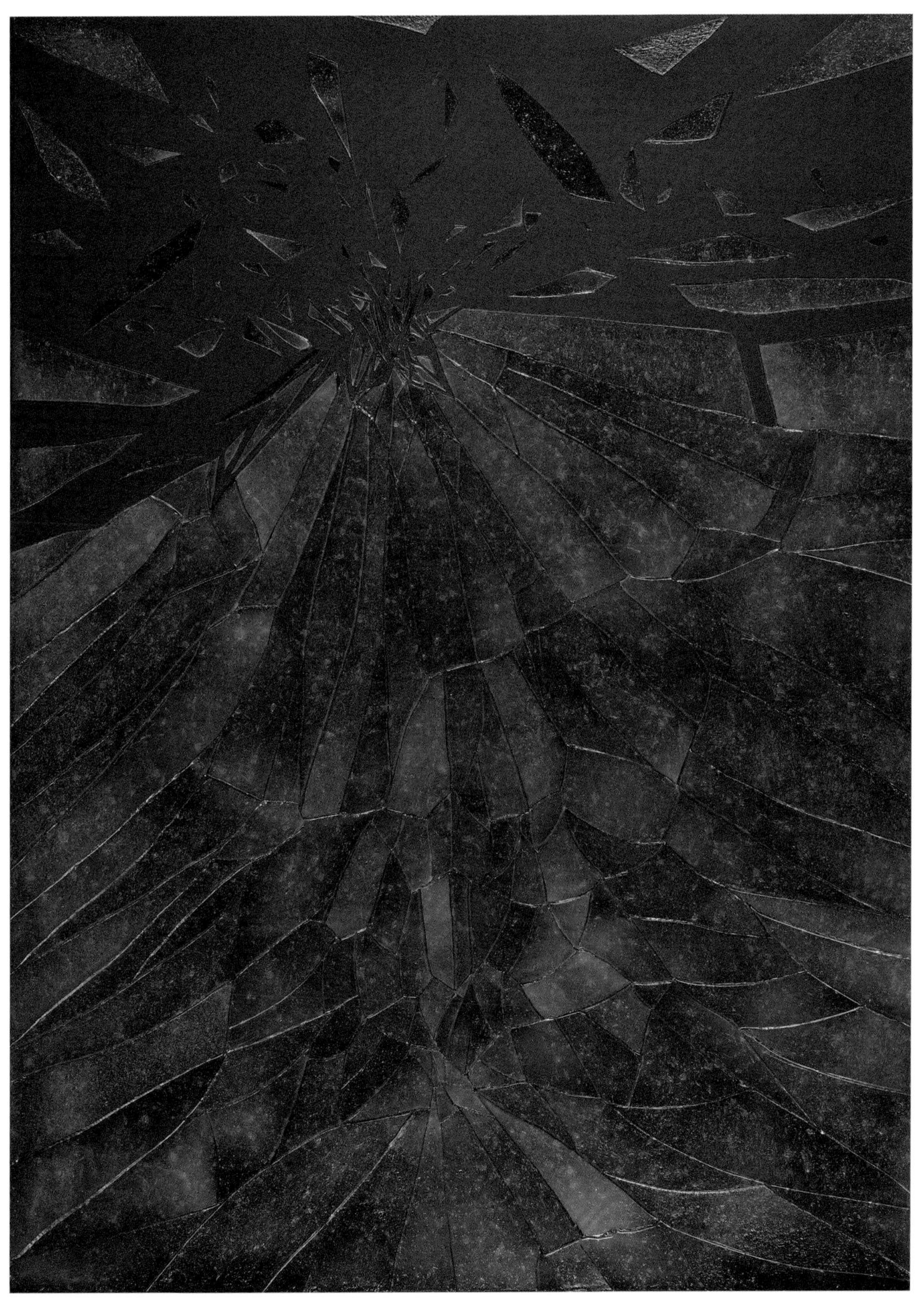

Untitled / Melancholia series
2019
Acrylic and heavy gel on canvas
210 × 155 cm

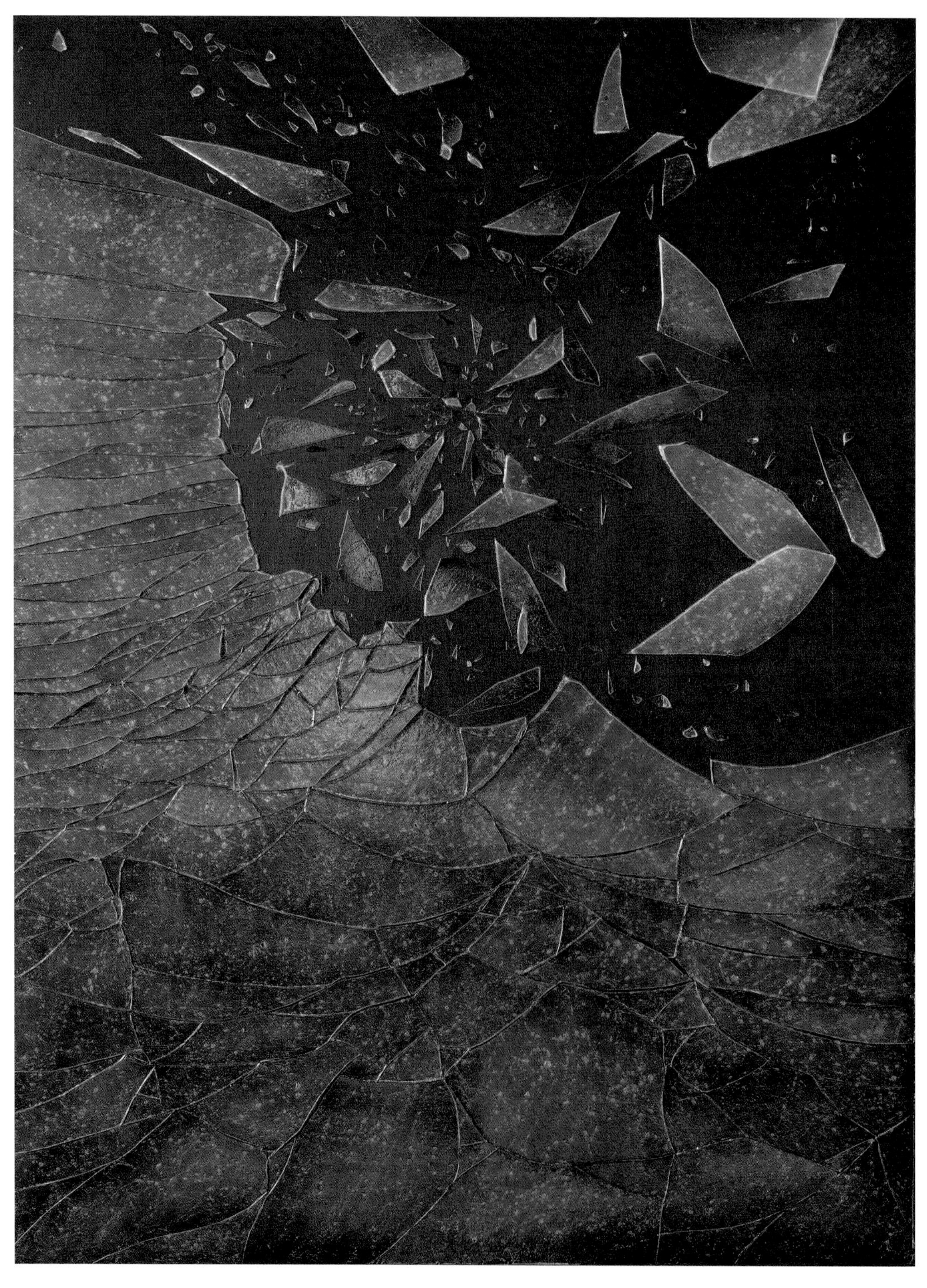

Untitled / *Melancholia* series
2019
Acrylic and heavy gel on canvas
200 × 150 cm

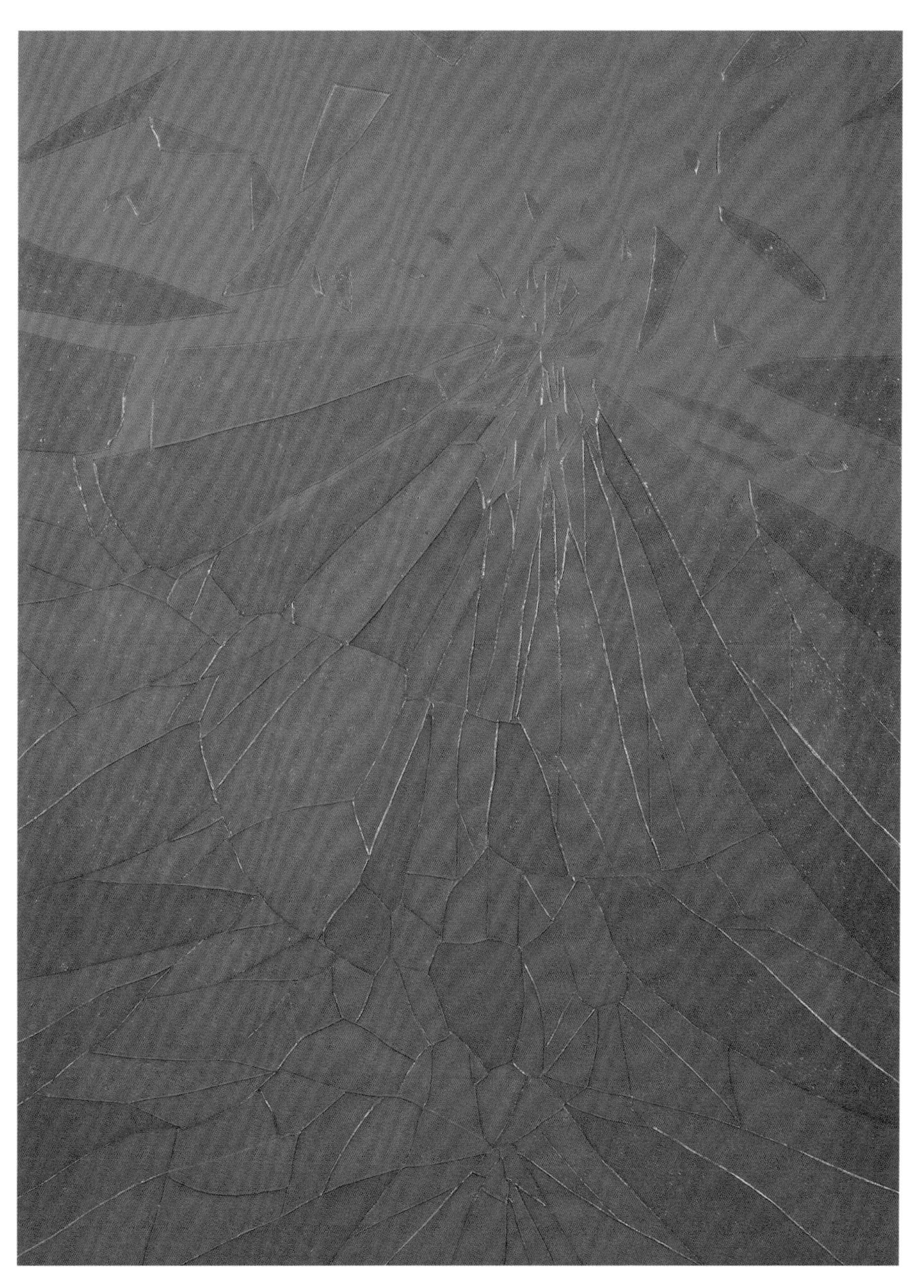

Untitled / *Melancholia* series
2020
Acrylic and heavy gel on canvas
150 × 110 cm

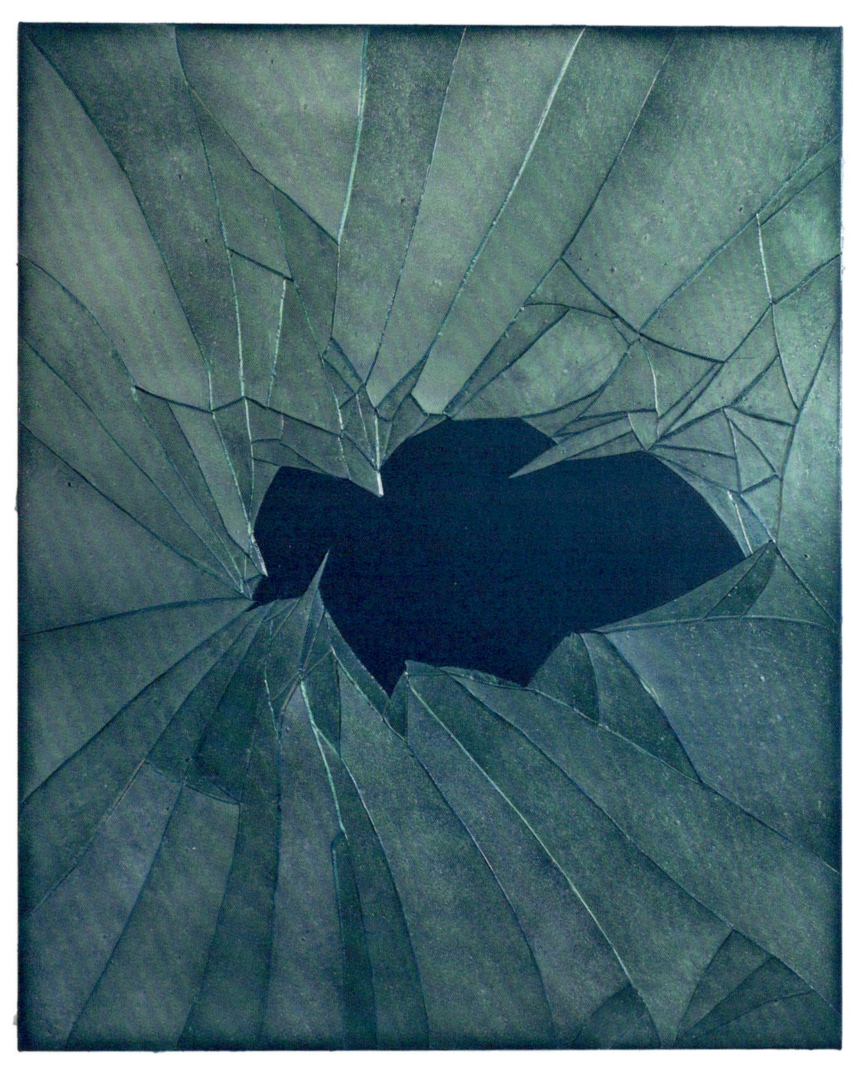

Untitled / Melancholia series
2021
Acrylic and heavy gel on canvas
120 × 100 cm

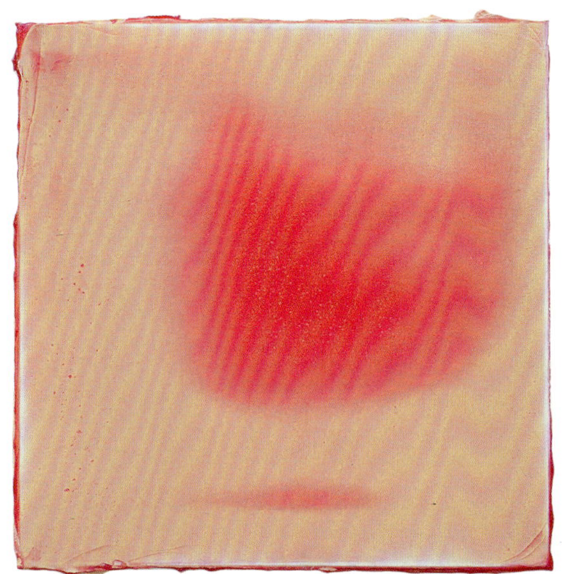

Nefs 18 / *Nefs* series
2014
Acrylic and heavy gel on canvas
35 × 35 cm

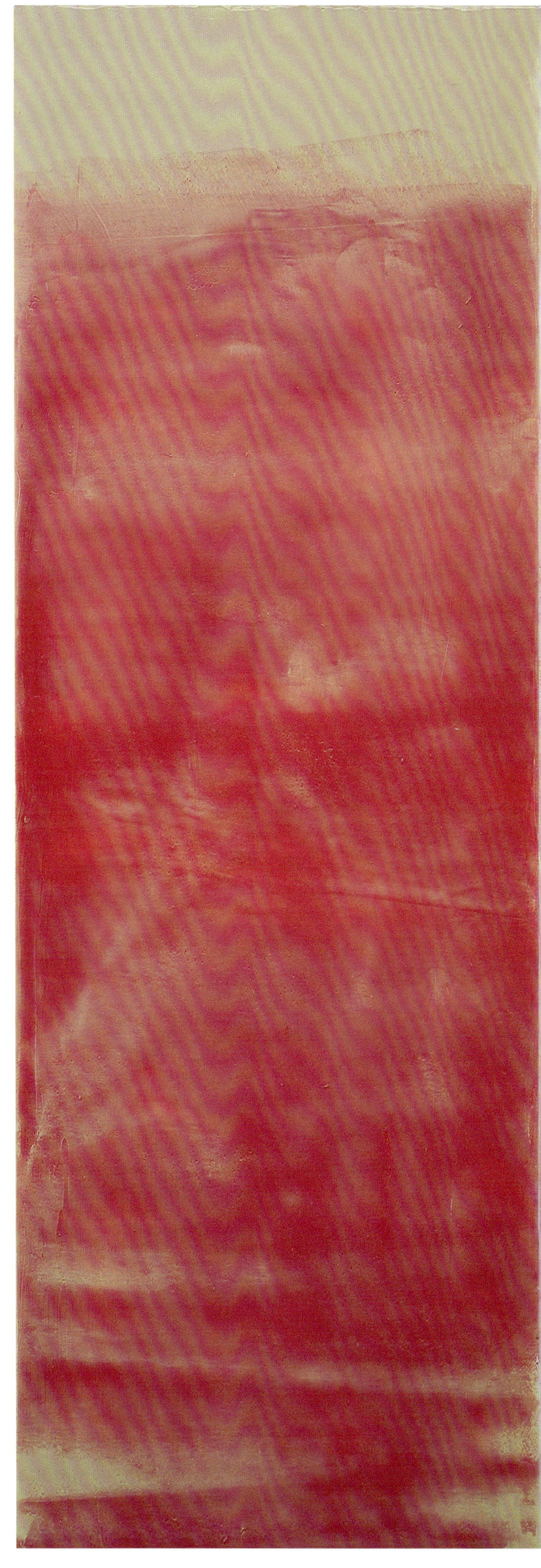

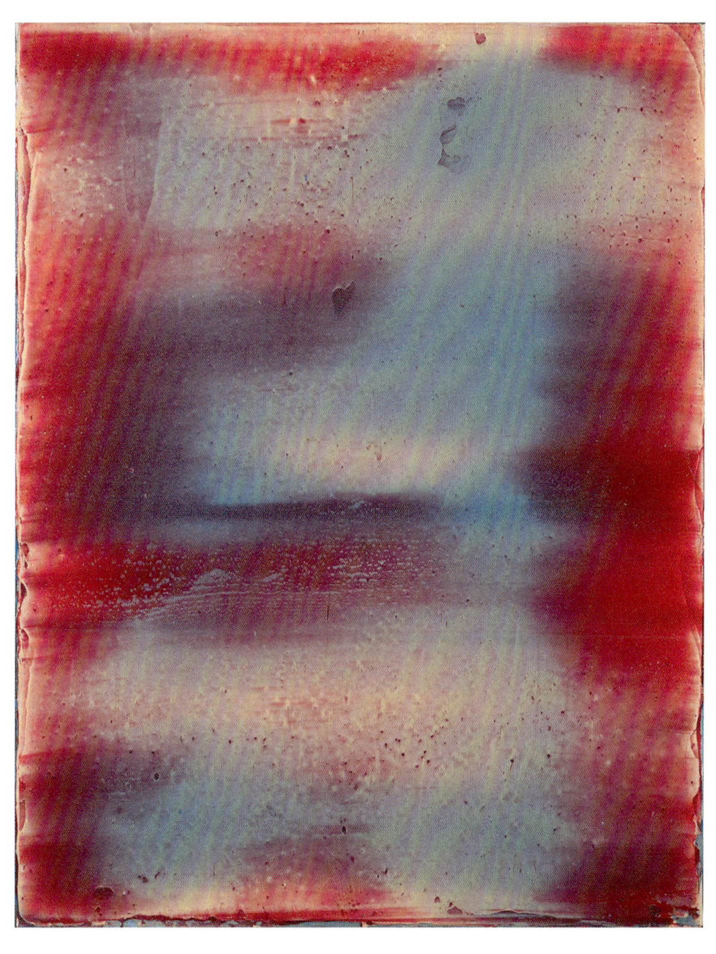

Nefs 3 / *Nefs* series
2014
Acrylic and heavy gel on canvas
290 × 100 cm

Untitled / *Nefs* series
2016
Acrylic and heavy gel on canvas
90 × 70 cm

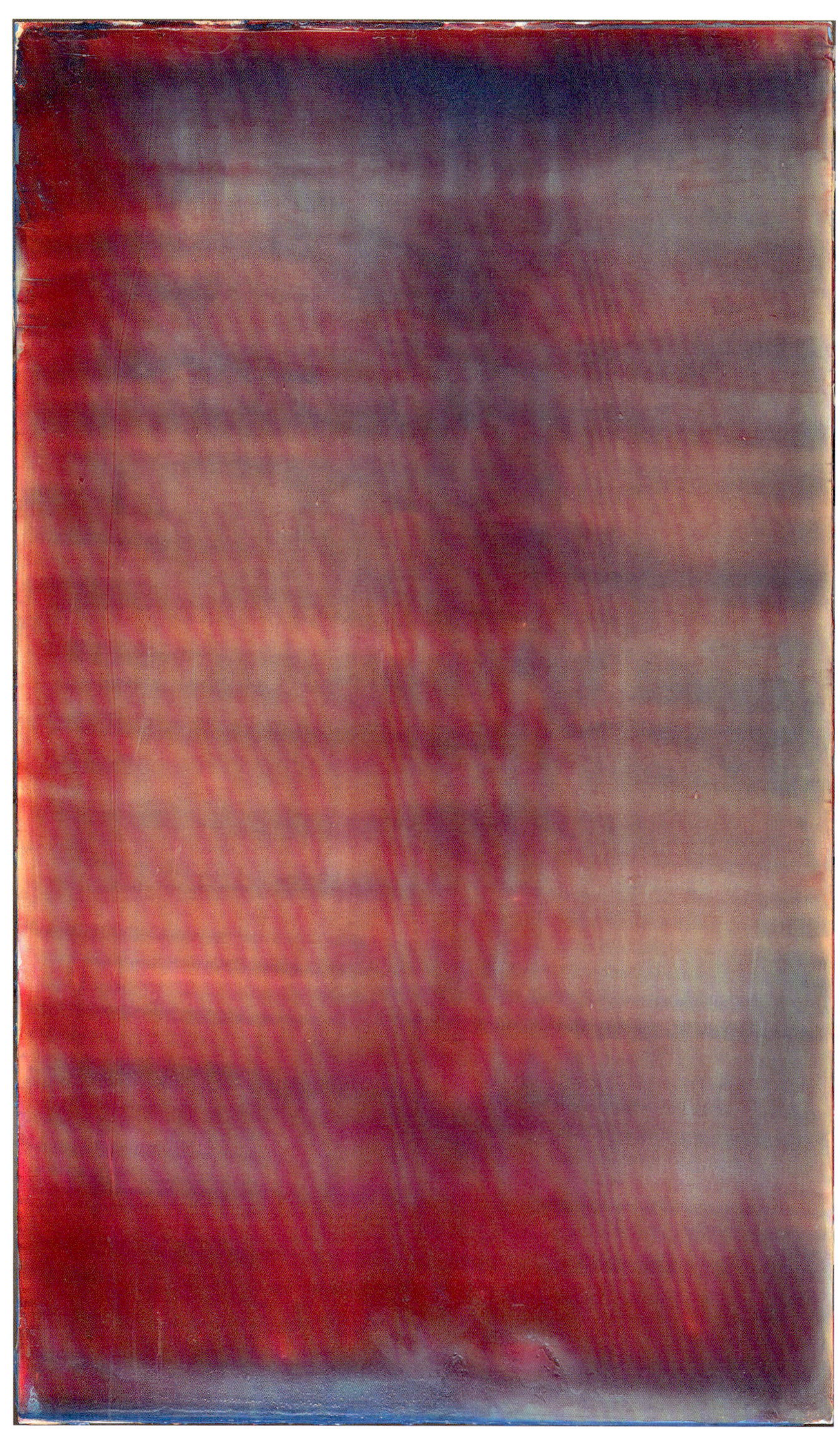

Nefs 1 / Nefs series
2014
Acrylic and heavy gel on canvas
200 × 120 cm

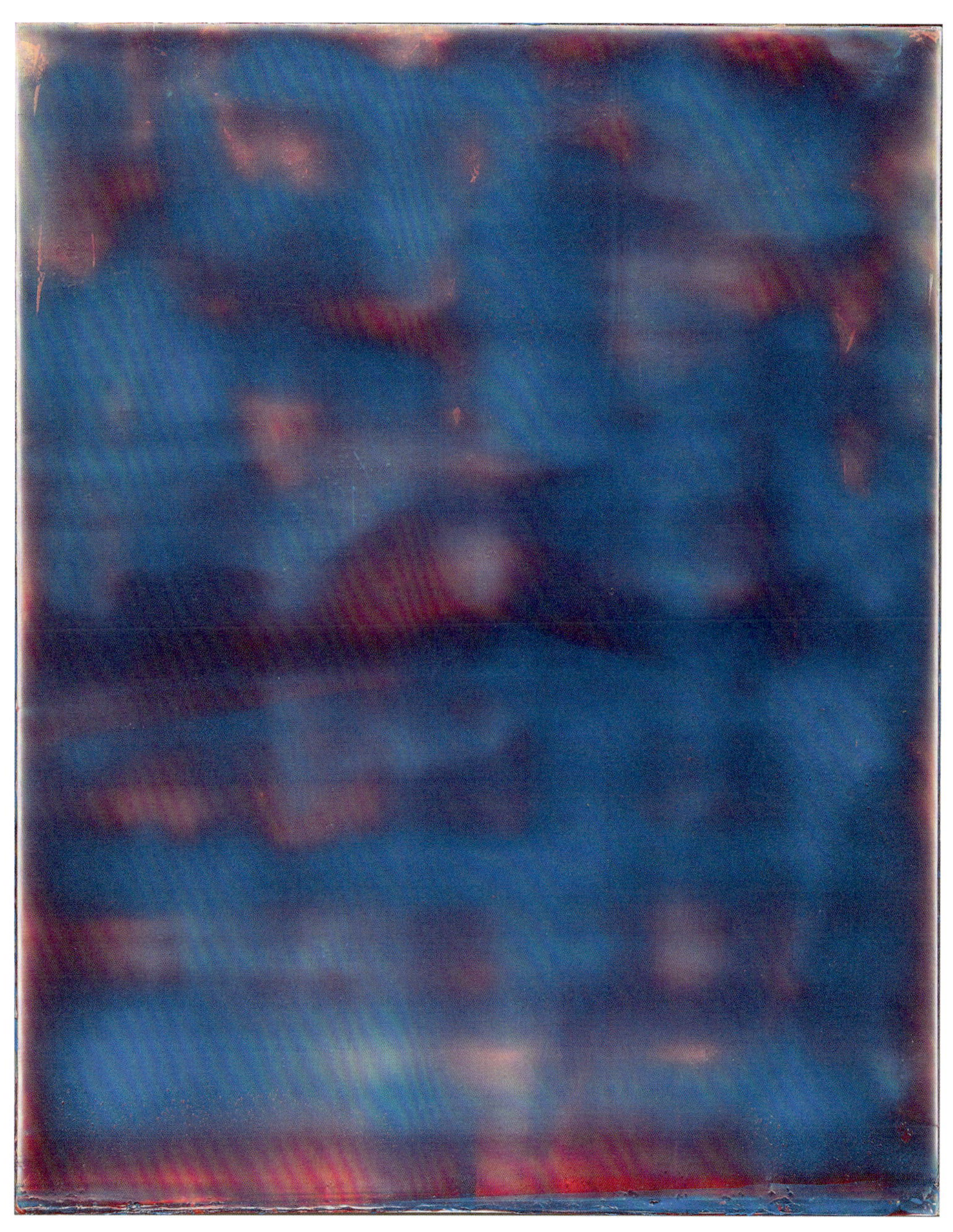

Untitled / Nefs series
2014
Acrylic and heavy gel on canvas
150 × 120 cm

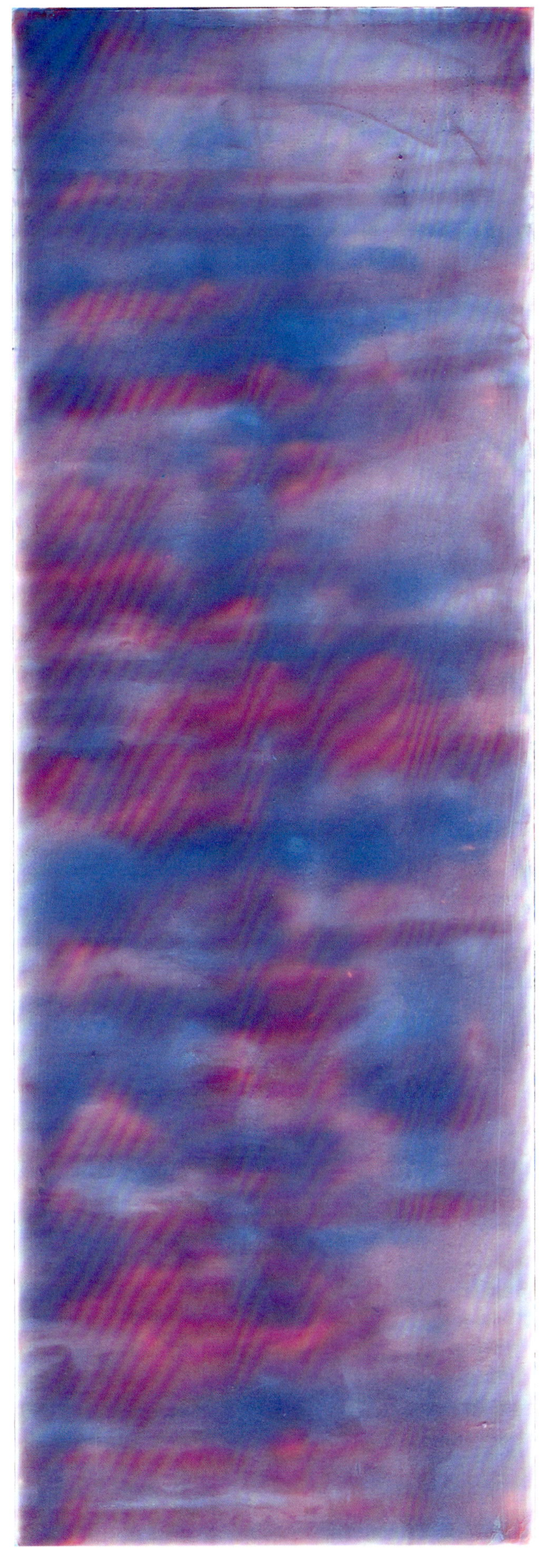

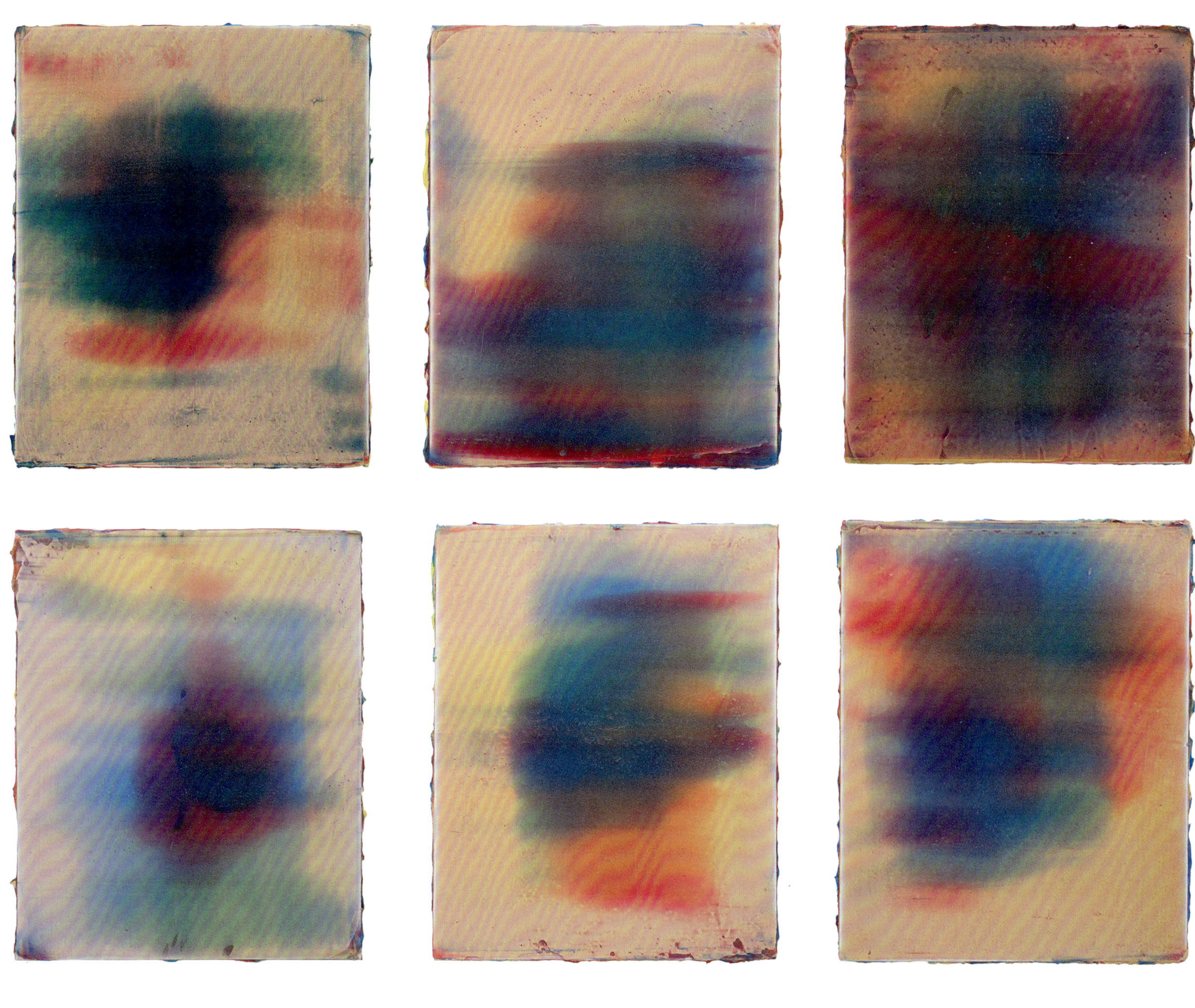

Nefs 2 / Nefs series
2014
Acrylic and heavy gel on canvas
290 × 100 cm

Untitled / Nefs series
2014
Acrylic and heavy gel on canvas
Group of 6 works, 55 × 45 cm each

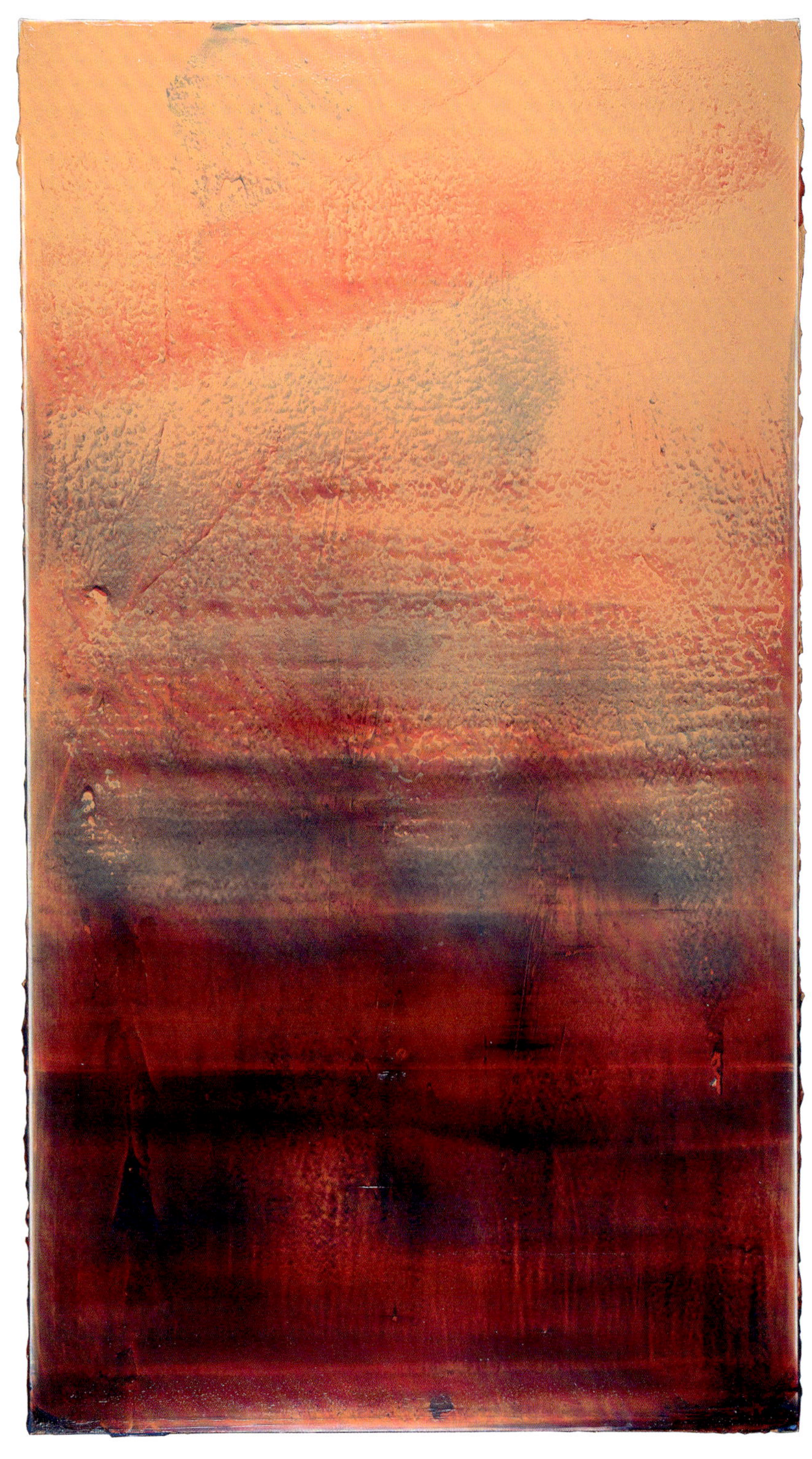

Untitled / Nefs series
2021
Acrylic and heavy gel on canvas
185 × 106 cm

Wound / Nefs series
2016
Acrylic and heavy gel on canvas
103 × 88 cm

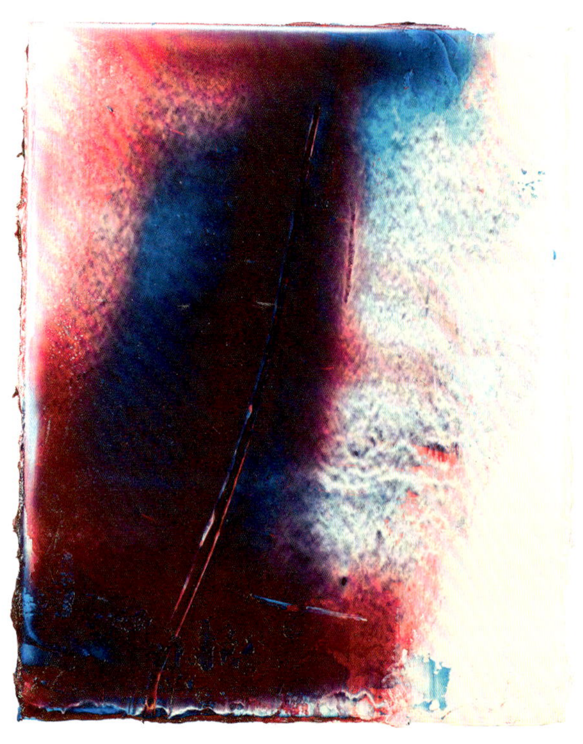

Wound / Nefs series
2020
Acrylic and heavy gel on canvas
50 × 40 cm

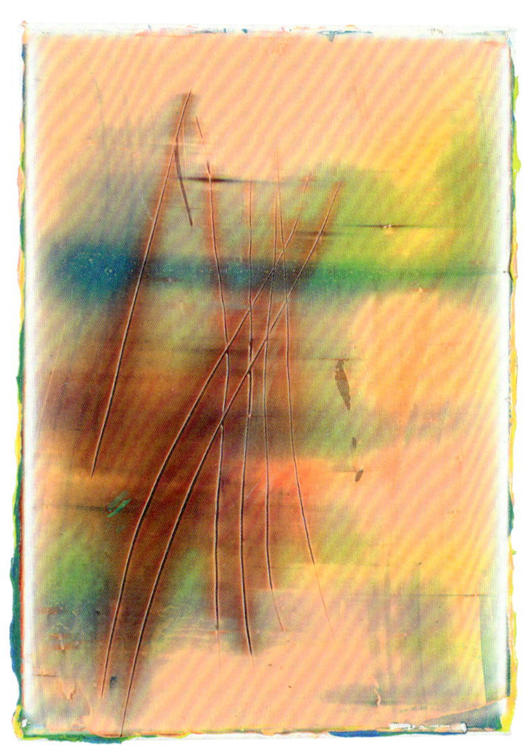 

Wound / Nefs series
2018
Acrylic and heavy gel on canvas
40 × 28 cm

Wound / Nefs series
2018
Acrylic and heavy gel on canvas
40 × 28 cm

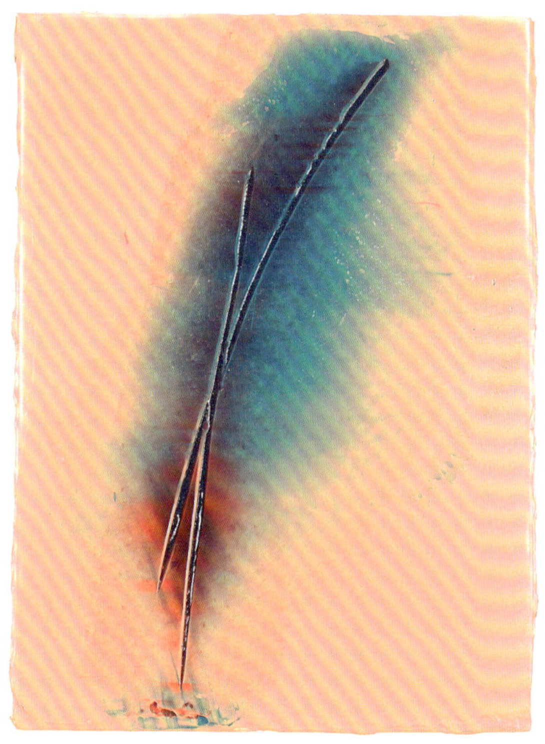

Wound / Nefs series
2020
Acrylic and heavy gel on canvas
40 × 30 cm

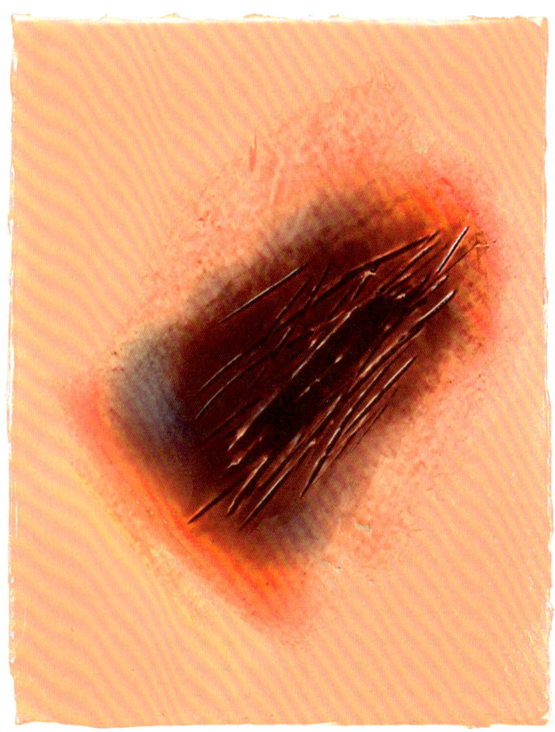

Wound / Nefs series
2020
Acrylic and heavy gel on canvas
40 × 32 cm

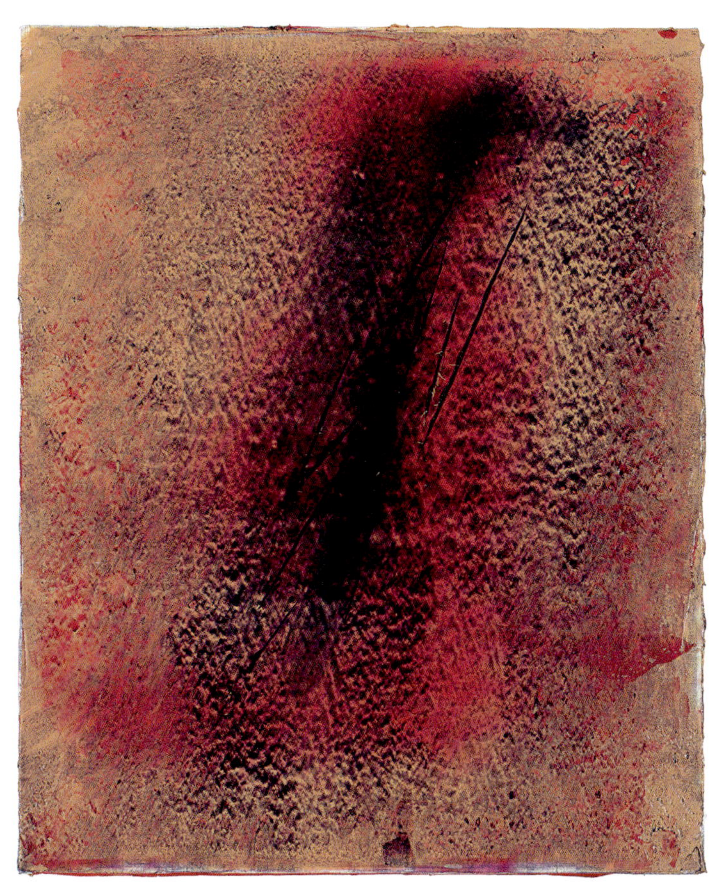

Wound / Nefs series
2021
Acrylic and heavy gel on canvas
60 × 50 cm

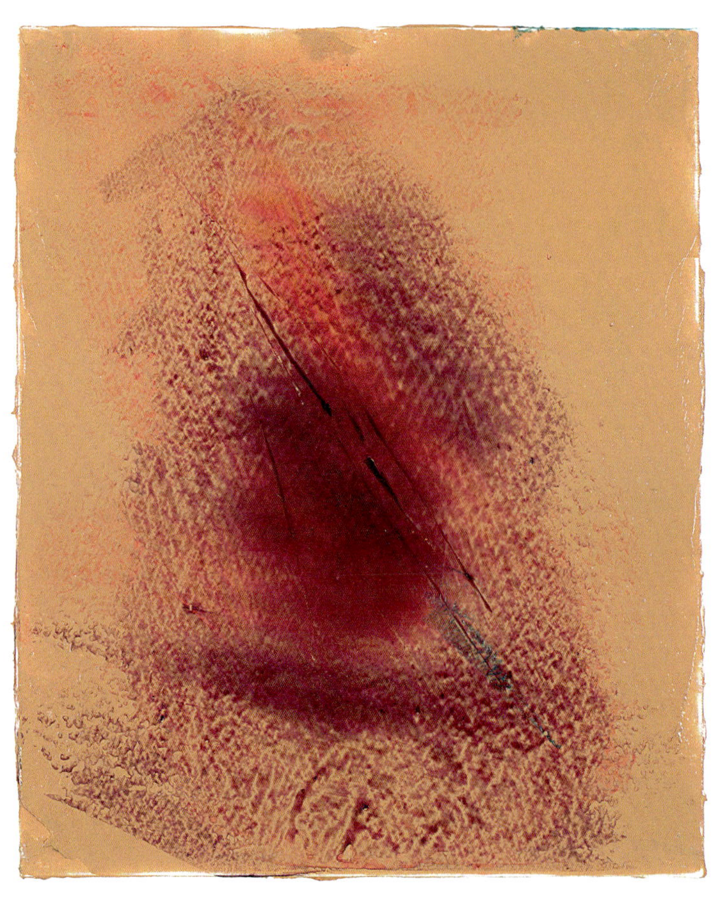

Wound / Nefs series
2021
Acrylic and heavy gel on canvas
60 × 50 cm

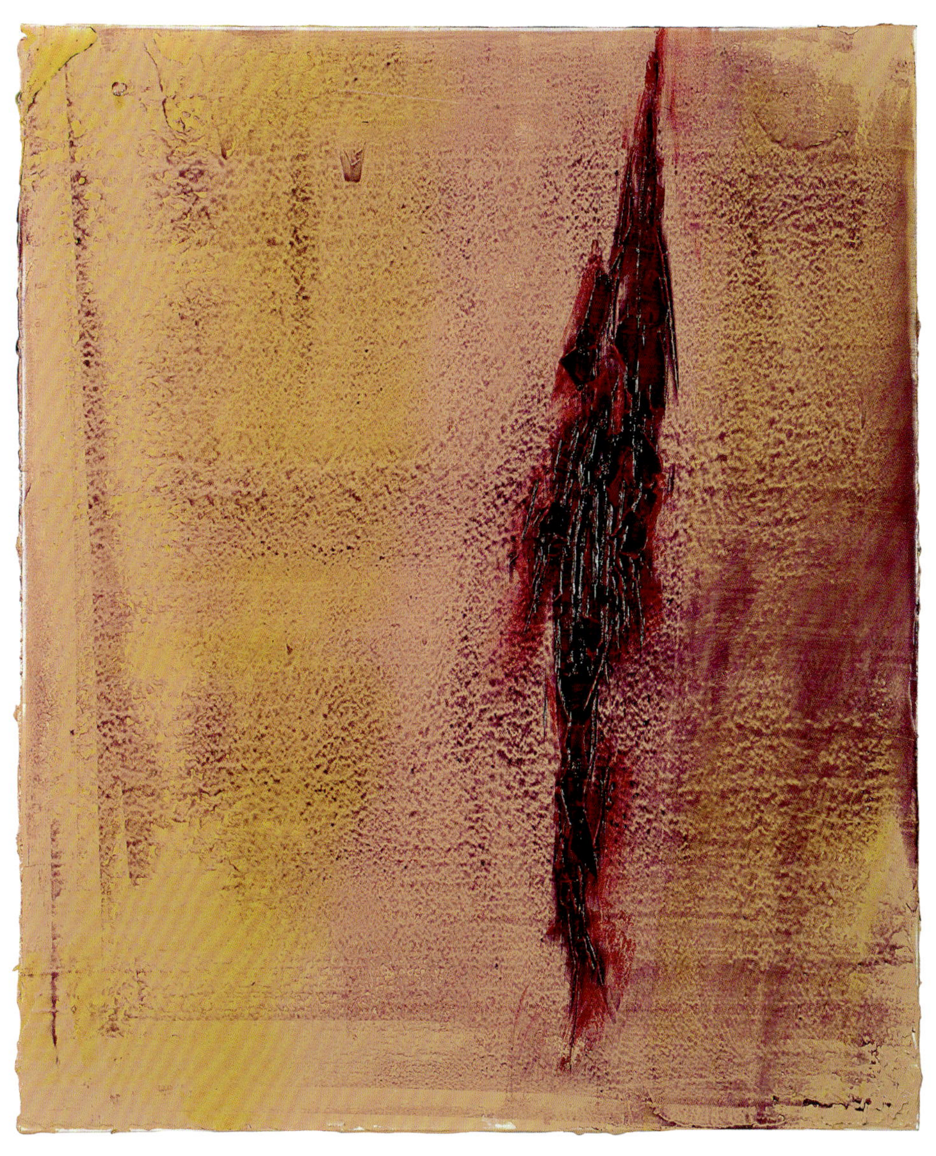

Wound / Nefs series
2021
Acrylic and heavy gel on canvas
120 × 100 cm

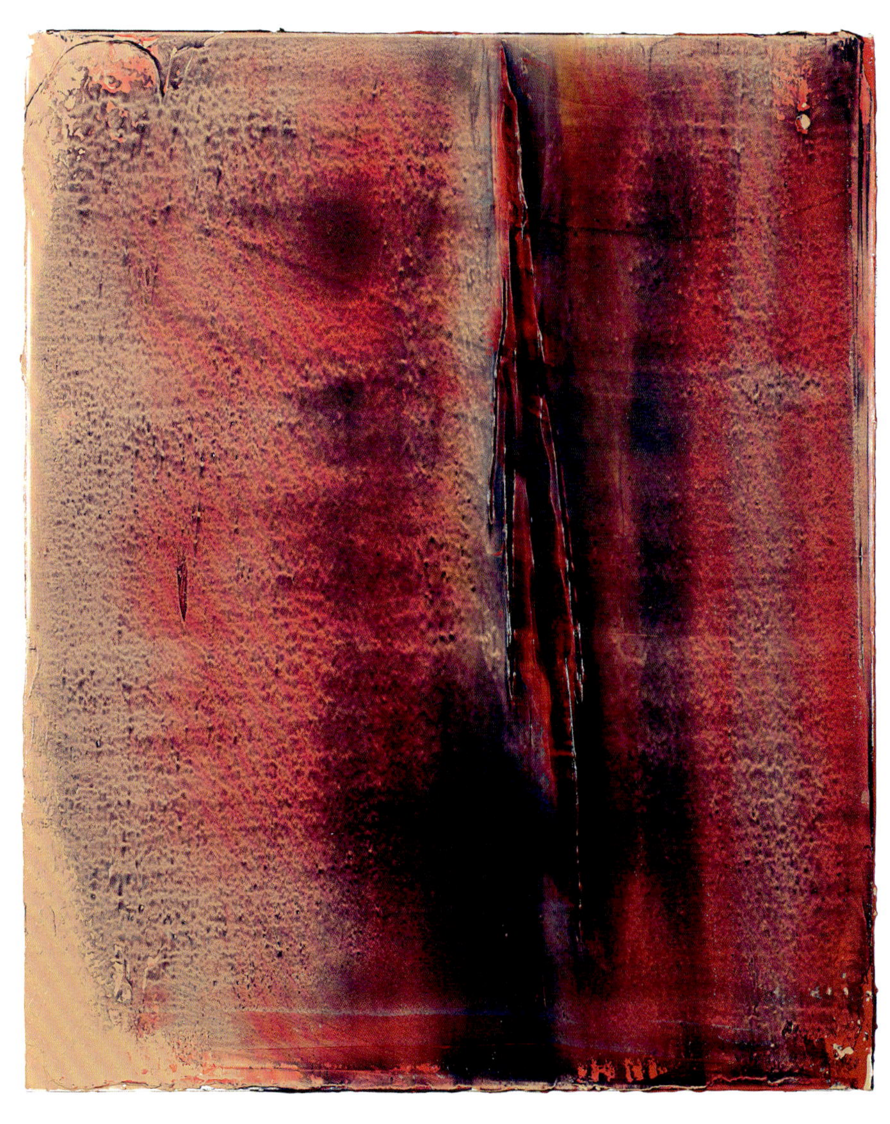

Wound / *Nefs* series
2021
Acrylic and heavy gel on canvas
120 × 100 cm

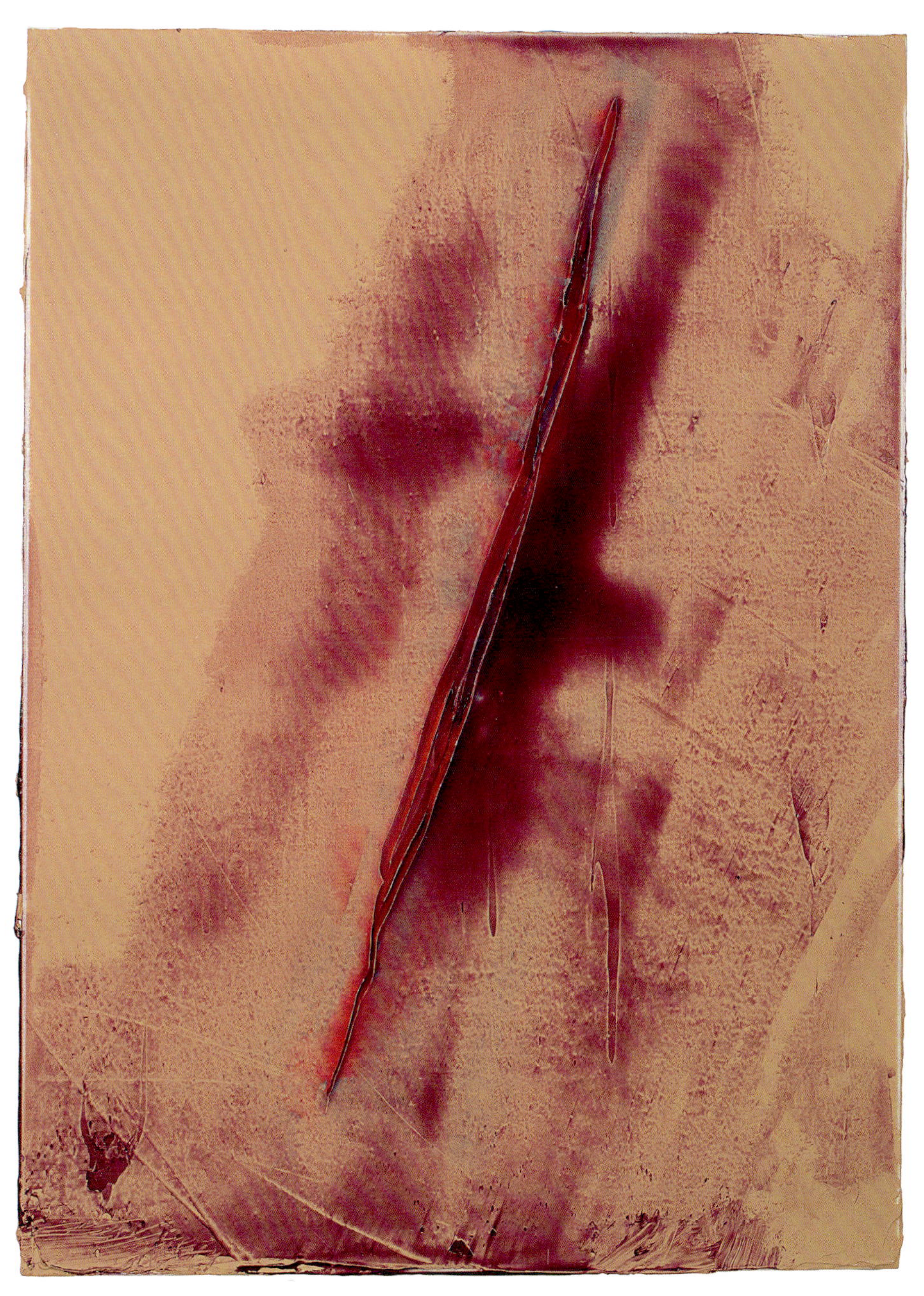

Wound / Nefs series
2021
Acrylic and heavy gel on canvas
150 × 100 cm

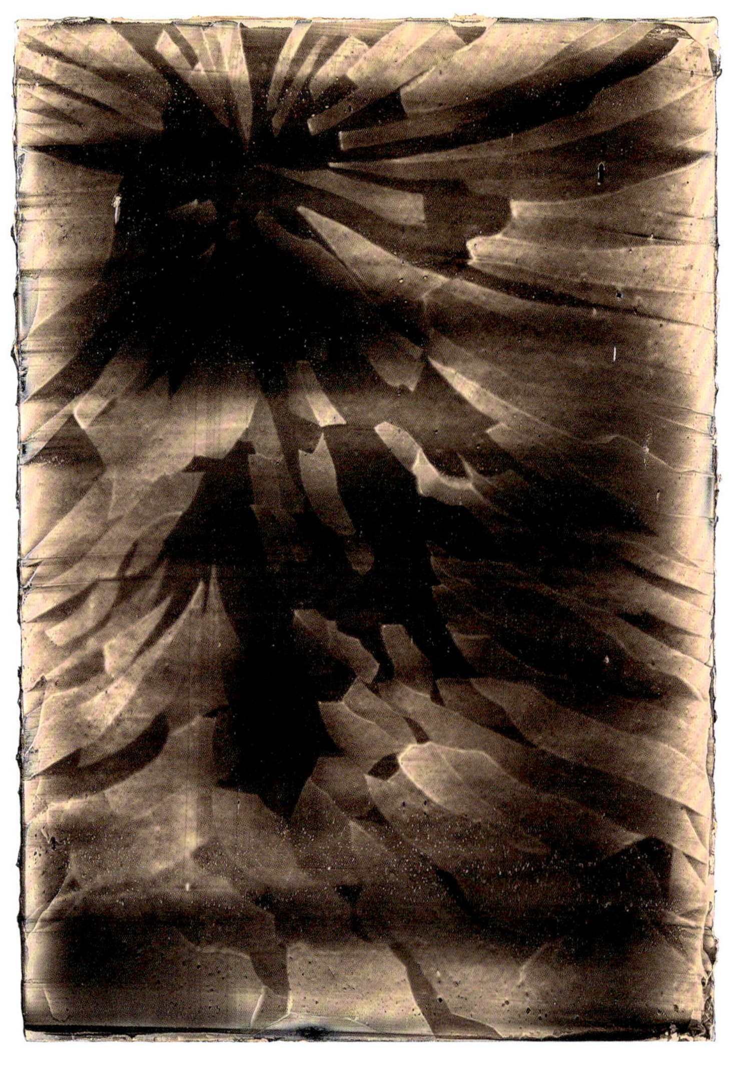

Nefs & Melancholia / Catharsis
series
2020
Acrylic and heavy gel on canvas
100 × 70 cm

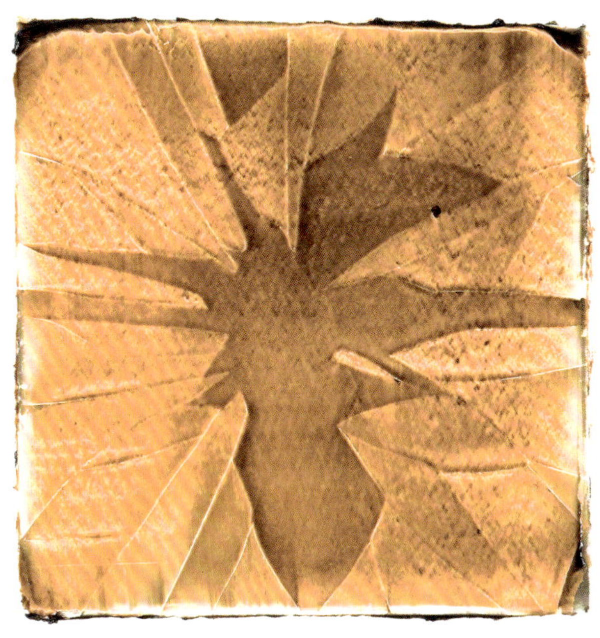

Untitled / *Catharsis* series
2020
Acrylic and heavy gel on canvas
50 × 50 cm

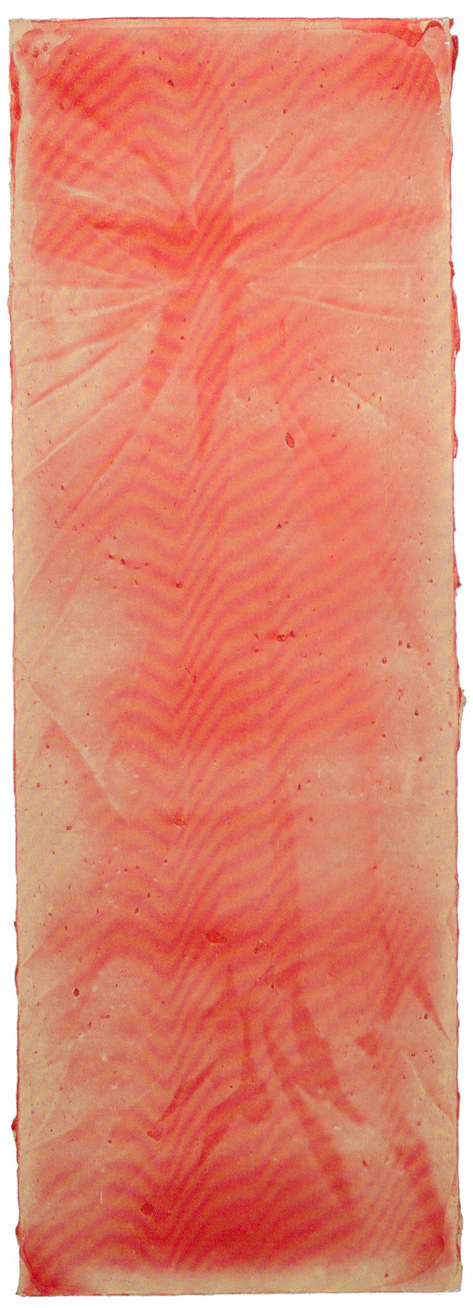

Untitled / Catharsis series
2016
Acrylic and heavy gel on canvas
117 × 42 cm

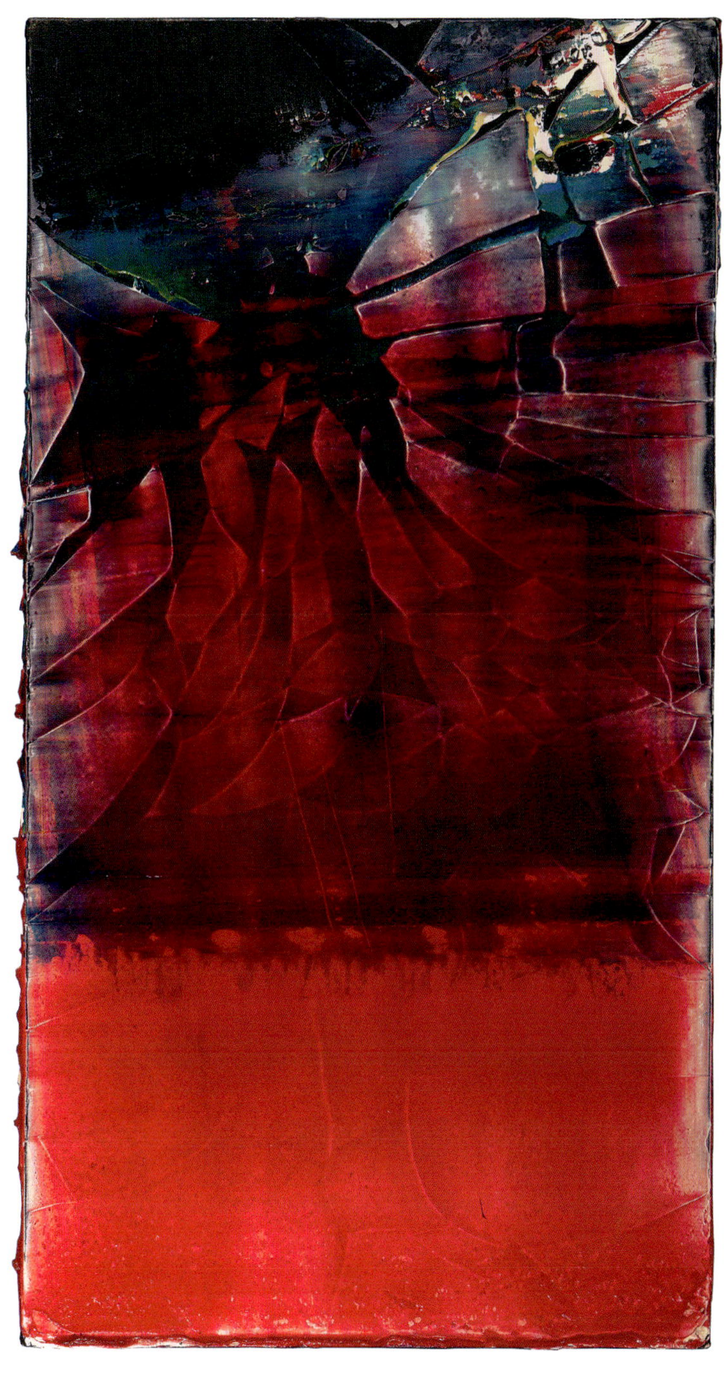

Untitled / *Catharsis* series
2020
Acrylic and heavy gel on canvas
130 × 60 cm

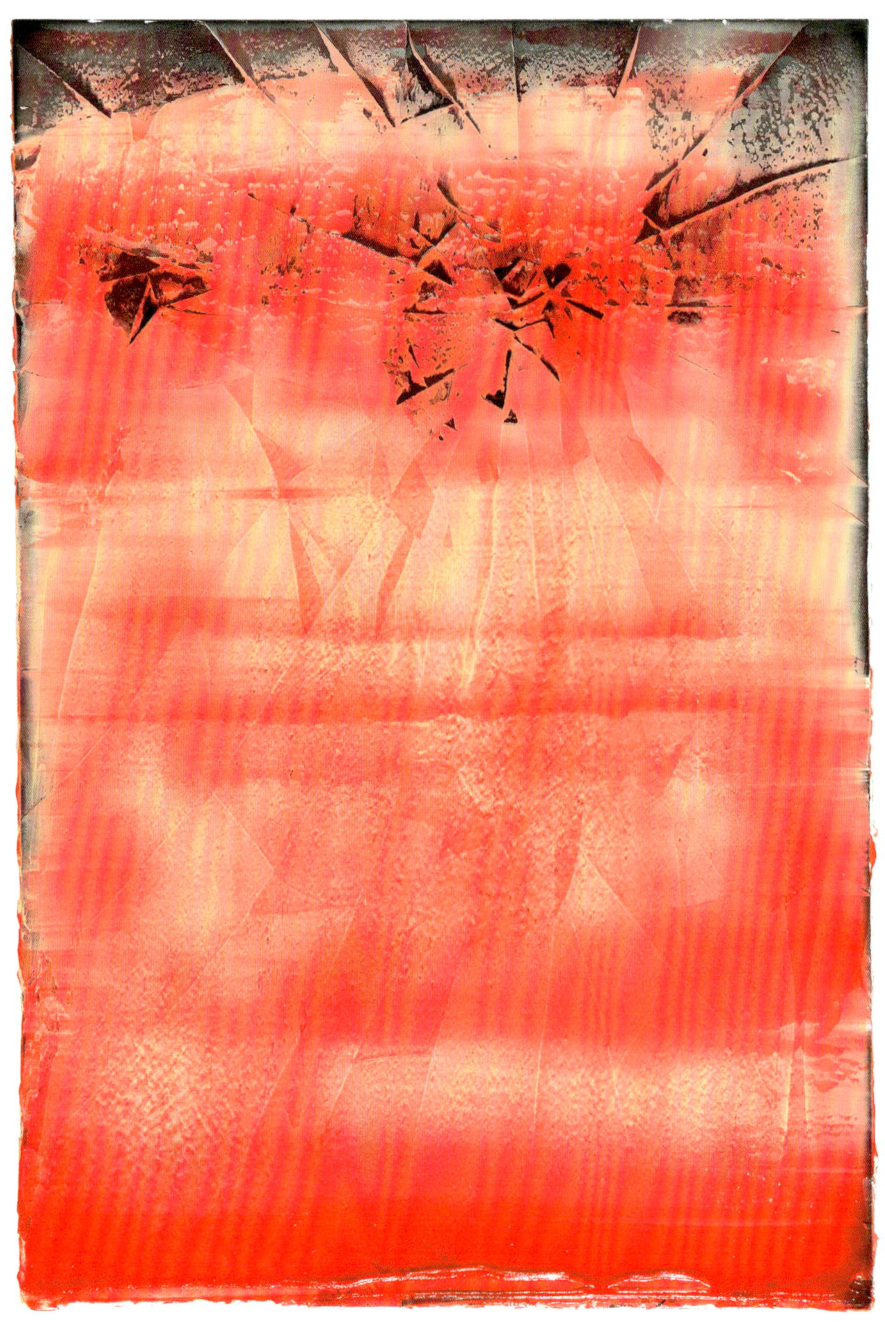

Untitled / *Catharsis* series
2020
Acrylic and heavy gel on canvas
160 × 110 cm

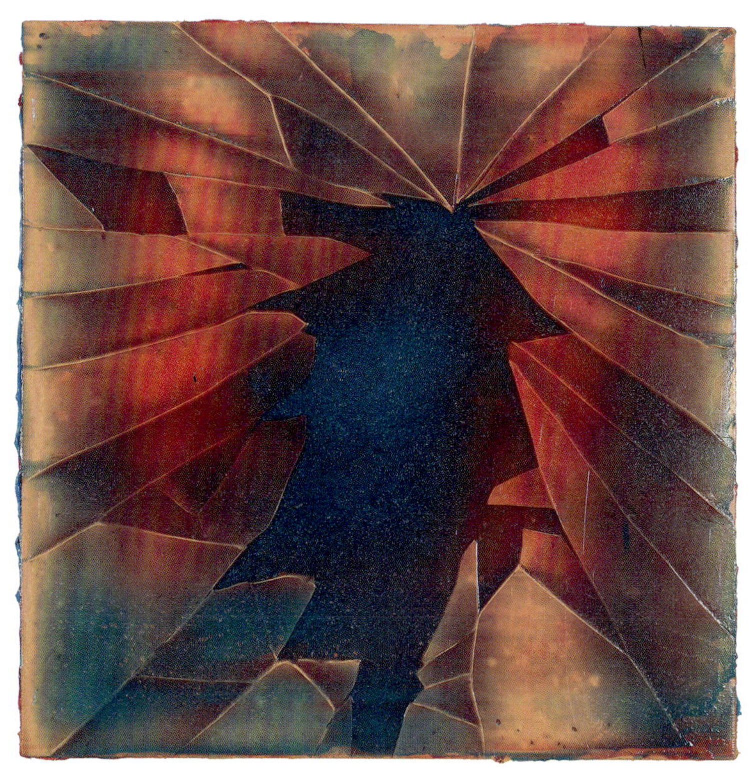

Untitled / Catharsis series
2021
Acrylic and heavy gel on canvas
60 × 60 cm

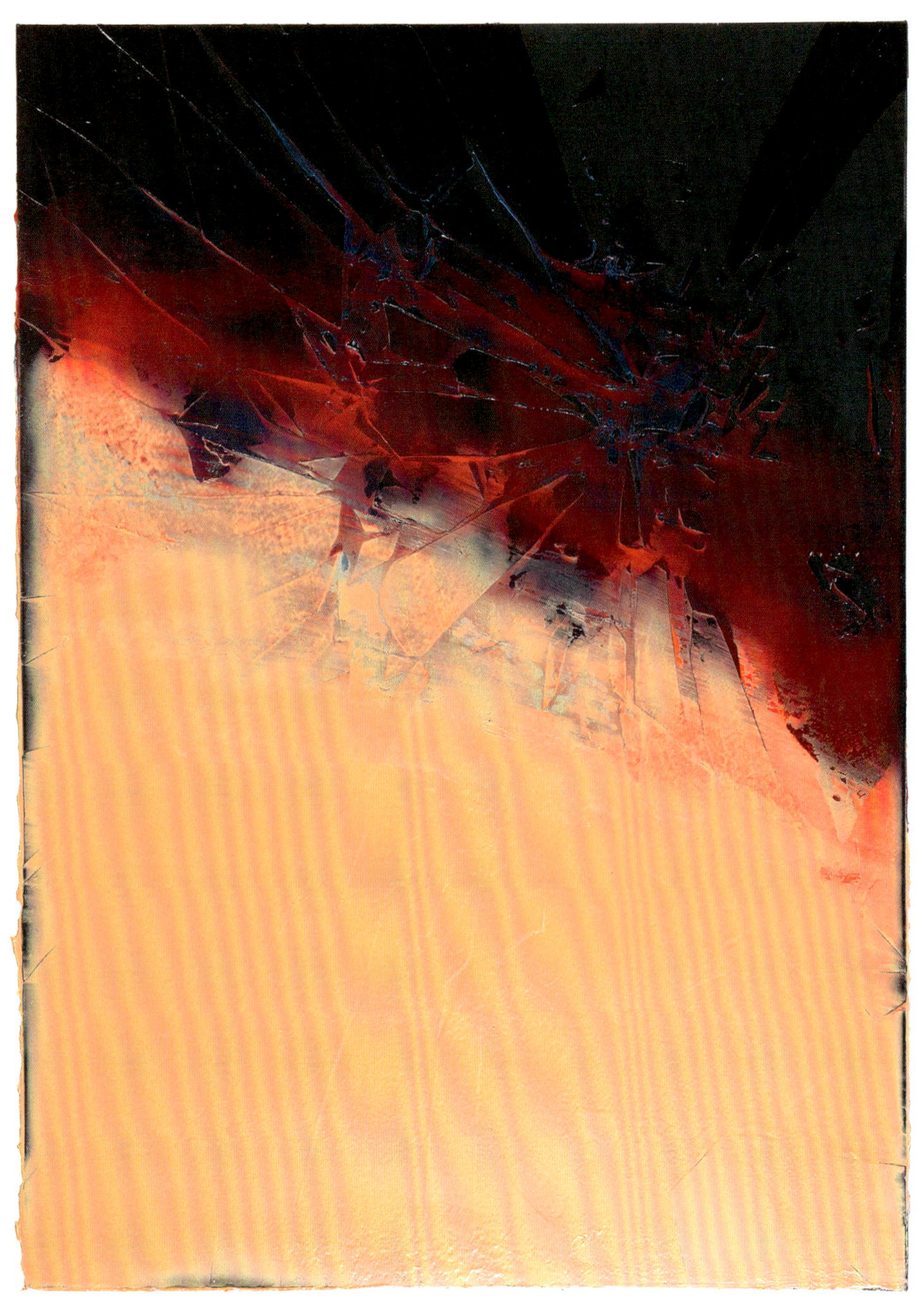

Untitled / Catharsis series
2020
Acrylic and heavy gel on canvas
180 × 130 cm

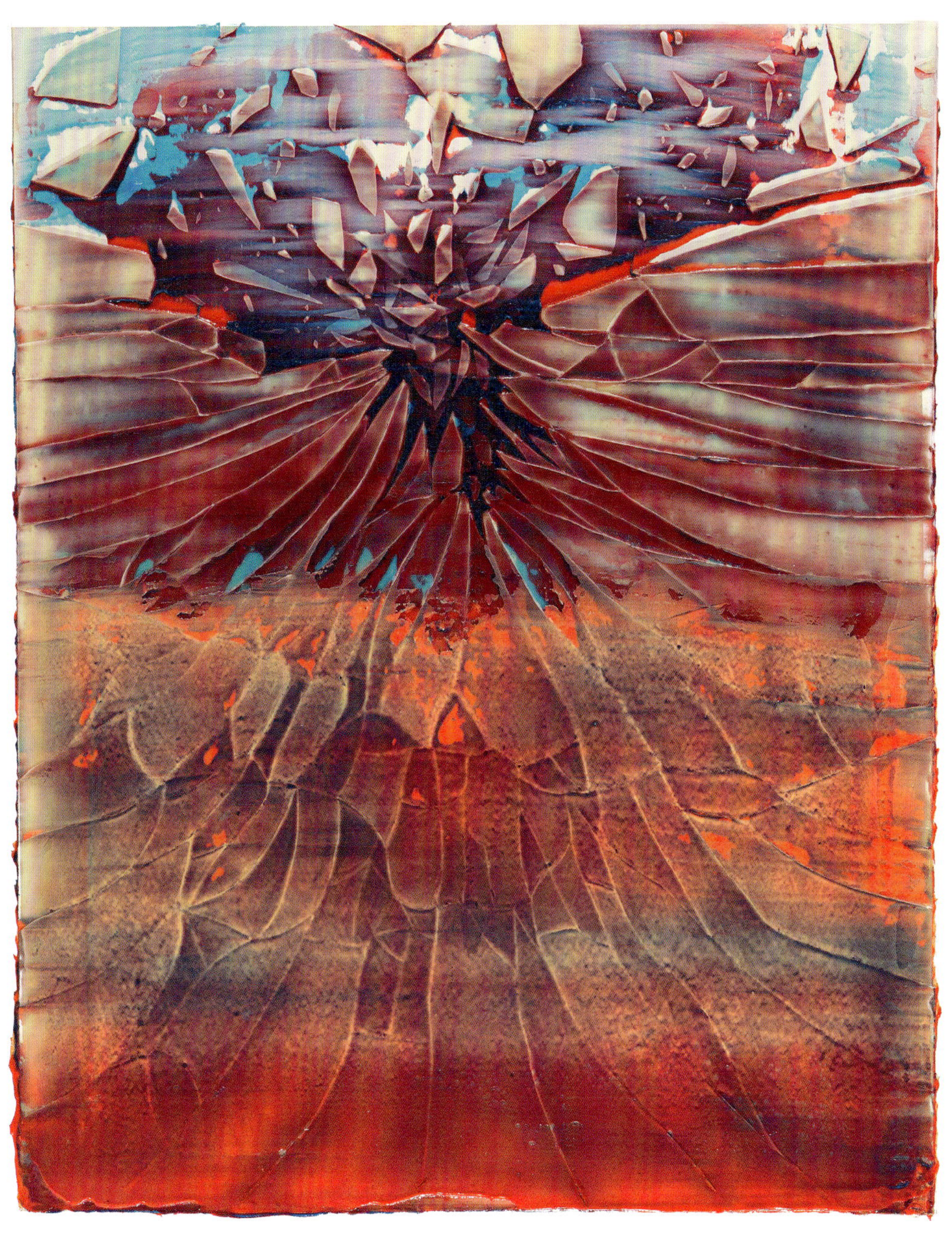

Untitled / Catharsis series
2021
Acrylic and heavy gel on canvas
150 × 120 cm

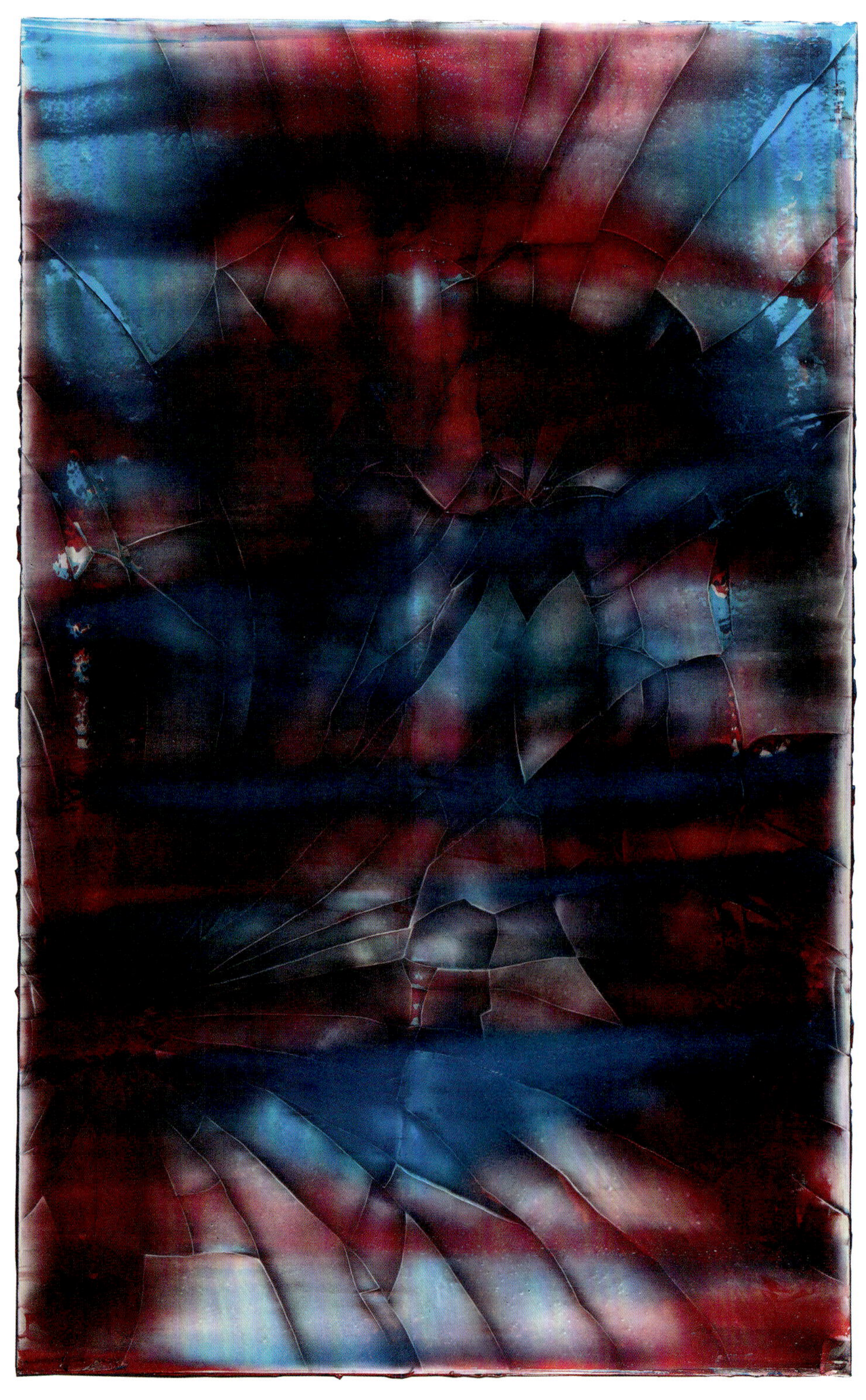

Untitled / Catharsis series
2021
Acrylic and heavy gel on canvas
220 × 140 cm

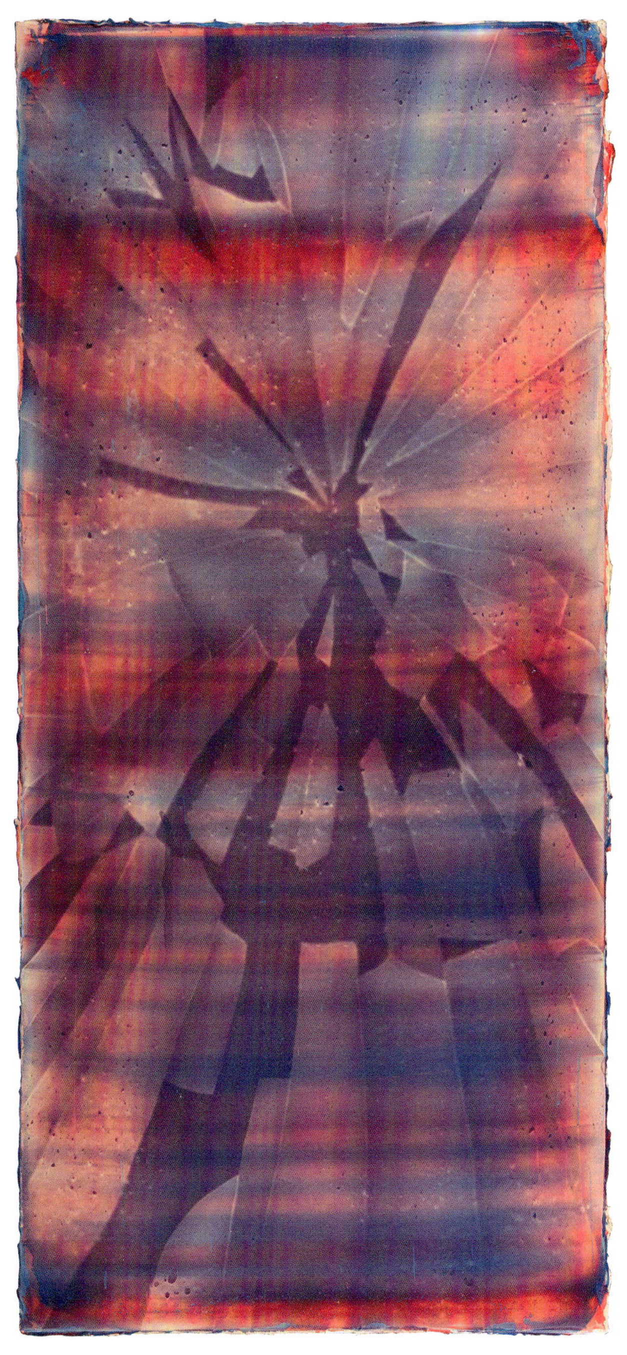

Untitled / Catharsis series
2021
Acrylic and heavy gel on canvas
129 × 60 cm

Biography and Exhibitions

Nejat Satı graduated from the Painting Department of Dokuz Eylül Fine Arts University, İzmir in 2004. Since then, his work has been shown in solo exhibitions both in and out of Turkey, and is represented in numerous private and corporate collections worldwide. Satı has developed a technique that reflects the spiritual and material zeitgeist of our age. He has created an abstract painting language that becomes plastic on the surface of the canvas, thanks to the unique combination of the gel medium and acrylic paint. Moreover, he did not hesitate to let go of the brush at times, giving way to other tools with which he adopted a more dynamic attitude where the body plays an active role.

2004

• *The Nude Who Abandons His Location*, K2 Sanat Merkezi, İzmir, Group Exhibition

• *Penthouse*, K2 Sanat Merkezi, İzmir, Group Exhibition

2005

• *Yeni Öneriler Yeni Önermeler 13*, Borusan Art Gallery, Group Exhibition. Curated by Ahu Antmen

• *Serbest Vuruş*, 9. İstanbul Bienali Misafirperverlik kapsamında, Group Exhibition. Curated by Halil Altındere

• *The Little, the Cheap, the Trash and Absolutely Passionate!*, K2 Sanat Merkezi, Helsinki, Group Exhibition

• *DERE&SATI, sanatçı portfolyo tanıtımı*, K2 Sanat Merkezi, İzmir, Group Exhibition

• *Others Change*, K2 Sanat Merkezi, İzmir, Group Exhibition

2006

• *Distilled / Sıradandan Yansıyanlar*, K2 Sanat Merkezi, İzmir, Group Exhibition. Curated by Philippine Hoegen and Sylvia Kouvali

2008

• *Today's Artist Istanbul Exhibition*, Akbank Sanat, Istanbul, Group Exhibition. Curated by Irina Batkova, Bart van der Heide, and Adnan Yıldız

2009

• *Yaratıcı Yıkım*, Outlet, Istanbul, Group Exhibition

• *Aferin*, Apartman Projesi, Solo Exhibition

• *Agora*, Sanatçının kendi atölyesi, İzmir, Solo Exhibition

2010

• *Hoşgeldin Noel*, Kızlarağası Hanı, İzmir, Group Exhibition

• *İddalıyız*, 46A, İzmir, Group Exhibition

• *Sessizlik, Fırtına*, Tütün Deposu, İzmir, Group Exhibition. Curated by Necmi Sönmez

• *Fikirler Suça Dönüşünce*, Depo, Istanbul, Group Exhibition. Curated by Halil Altındere

• *Dil Altı*, Pi Artworks, Istanbul, Solo Exhibition

2011

• *Doğa Cennetse Kent Cehennemdir*, Cer Modern, Ankara, Group Exhibition. Curated by Yaygara Topluluğu

• *Artbeat*, Pi Artworks, Istanbul, Group Exhibition

• *Drugstore*, art ON, Istanbul, Solo Exhibition

2012

• *Otoportre*, Alanistanbul, Istanbul,
Group Exhibition. Curated by
Efe Korkut Kurt
• *Pi @ Q*, Q Temporary, Beyrut
Lübnan
• *Encounters: Turkish Contemporary
Art in Korea*, Araart, Seul, Güney
Kore, Group Exhibition. Curated by
Hasan Bülent Kahraman
• *Organic Abstract*, Pi Artworks,
Istanbul, Solo Exhibition
• *Halet-i Ruhiye*, Pi Artworks, Istanbul,
Solo Exhibition

2013

• *Hot Spot Istanbul*, Haus Konstruktiv,
Zurich, Group Exhibition

2014

• *Soyutla Başlamak*, Kare Art Gallery,
Istanbul, Group Exhibition
• *The Feeling of Happiness*, Homa
Art Gallery, Tehran İran, Group
Exhibition. Curated by Saeed Ensafi
• *Istanbul Art Scene*, Yallay Gallery,
Hong Kong, Solo Exhibition
• *Nefs*, Pi Artworks, Istanbul,
Solo Exhibition

2015

• *Breathe*, Kare Art Gallery, Istanbul,
Group Exhibition
• *Fuck You Modernity*, Artnivo, Lucca,
Istanbul, Solo Exhibition

2016

• *Cracks*, Pi Artworks London,
 Solo Exhibition
• *Mastürbasyon*, Mixer, Istanbul,
Group Exhibition
• *Formun Gücü*, Plato Sanat, Istanbul,
Group Exhibition. Curated by
Marcus Graf
• *O Zaman Renk!*, Artnivo, Istanbul,
Group Exhibition. Curated by Selen
Sarıoğlu

2017

• *Yeni Nejat Eczanesi*, Ins By Periferi,
Istanbul, Solo Exhibition
• *Karanlıktaki Işık*, Pi Artworks,
Istanbul, Solo Exhibition
• Artist Residency, Ateliers Höherweg
271, Düsseldorf

2018

• *Yeni Nejat Eczanesi 2*, Tab Gallery,
Istanbul, Solo Exhibition

2019

• *Wild Flowers*, Pi Artworks, Istanbul,
Solo Exhibition
• *Common Puppy*, Shelter Artist
Run Space, İzmir, Solo Exhibition

Author Biographies

Necmi Sönmez

studied art history at the universities of Mainz, Paris, Newcastle, and Frankfurt, and received his PhD from Johann Wolfgang Goethe University on Wolfgang Laib (2000).

After working as curatorial associate at Museum Wiesbaden and Museum moderner Kunst Stiftung Ludwig, Vienna, he served as Curator for Contemporary Art at Museum Folkwang, Essen (2001–5).

After working at Kunsthochschule Kassel, he became Artistic Director of Kunstverein Arnsberg (2005–8) and member of the Acquisition Committee at FRAC Franche-Comté (2005–8). He established the artists' residency program ArtCenter Istanbul (2009–14), as well as many long-term exhibition projects for Borusan Contemporary.

He has independently carried out several cooperation-based curatorial projects and residency programs internationally, and has worked as an adjunct tutor/curator at various museums, including Tate, Staatliche Museen zu Berlin, Kiasma, Deutsche Bank KunstHalle, Kunstmuseum Bochum, Sabancı Museum, Elgiz Museum, Stiftung Zollverein, Essen, Antalya Kültür Sanat, Kunsthaus Göttingen. He is a regular contributor to *Unlimited* magazines and has published various texts in exhibition catalogs, as well as edited insert projects and handmade artist's books. Since 2015 he has collaborated with Skira editore, Milan, as an advising editor for monographic books on artists such as Murat Germen (2016), Kemal Seyhan (2018), and PG Thelander (2018).

Sabine Maria Schmidt

studied art history, musicology, and German language and literature in Germany and Spain. In 1997, she completed her doctoral thesis on "Eduardo Chillida: The Public Monuments." She maintains a continuous publication activity on twentieth- and twenty-first-century art, especially on video and media art, photography and art in the public space, and related image discourses and sociopolitical debates. She has edited several collective and monographic catalogs on artists, such as Cristina Lucas (Spain), Aernout Mik (Holland), Korps / Löffler (Germany), Christoph Faulhaber (Germany), and Runa Islam (Great Britain), and contributes regularly to art magazines and newspapers.

Since 1997 she has been working as a freelance and museum curator for Kunsthalle Bremen (1997–2000); Edith Russ Haus für Medienkunst, Oldenburg (2000); Wilhelm Lehmbruck Museum, Duisburg (2002–7); Museum Folkwang, Essen (2007–12); Kunsthalle Tübingen; and Kunstraum Düsseldorf. Since July 2019 she has served as Curator for Painting and Sculpture at Kunstsammlungen Chemnitz. She has curated over 60 shows internationally, in Birmingham (2007), Moscow (2008), Mexico City (2009/10), and Gdańsk (2014), among others. For the Kunstsammlungen Chemnitz, she conceived various collection presentations and, most recently, the comprehensive exhibition *Examination of a Case: Pop and Politics in Contemporary Textile Art*. In 2020, she co-curated the exhibition *The Price of the Future* for the new media art festival Pochen in Chemnitz. In 2021, she curated the extensive solo exhibition *Cristina Lucas: Immobile Engine*.